THE BIBLE ACCORDING TO

TRUMP

BRIAN CRAIG

Contents

Foreword 7

1. Thou shalt worship no other gods before me 15

2. Thou shalt not bow to any graven image......................31

3. Thou shalt not take the name of the lord in vain.......49

4. Thou shalt keep the sabbath holy 67

5. Honor thy father and thy mother................................87

6. Thou shalt not kill..99

7. Thou shalt not commit adultery 139

8. Thou shalt not steal.. 155

9. Thou shalt not bear false witness 191

10. Thou shalt not covet... 225

Epilogue... 247

Selected reading... 279

FOREWORD TO THE 2024 EDITION

'I think that I would be a great uniter. I think the world would unite if I were the leader of the United States.'

- Delusions 2:17

On May 30, 2024, Former President Donald John Trump was convicted by a New York jury on 34 counts felony counts related to falsifying business records. This was the first American president, sitting or former to have been charged with criminal offenses. Sentencing was set for early July, but waiting in the wings this election year, were also three other criminal trials in which the President was the principle suspect or co-conspirator: vote tampering conspiracies in Georgia, a federal election fraud case in Washington D.C and a federal charge of misappropriating government documents in a Florida court. The presumptive nominee for the Republican Party was elevated by voters who were fully aware he faced almost ninety criminal charges.

Four years on from the first edition and well into Mr Trump's third run for president, he hasn't changed and remains as dishonest as he was back when he descended a golden escalator, called immigrants a bunch of rapists and kicked off his campaign to become President of the United States. He used his first presidential term to enrich himself and his family, bilk the government out of millions, exacerbate international crises and to fiddle away while Rome burned, playing golf and watching himself on cable TV. He mishandled a deadly pandemic, leading to thousands more fatalities than necessary, and when he failed in his bid for reelection, lied about it, tried to stage a coup to stay in power and called on an angry mob to storm the Capitol and trash the place.

Since losing the election he has gone on a nationwide grievance tour, promoting the Big Lie that the election was rigged against him and stolen from his voters and finally wound up in court on multiple state and federal charges related to election fraud, campaign finance violations, stolen government documents and general financial malfeasance. Far from being the pious and decent leader his religious followers have deluded themselves into believing he is, Trump has kept breaking all the ten commandments the whole time has piled on new offences to most of them, which will be outlined in this edition.

This year he seeks the presidency again.

One would hope that as he seeks a second term against the man who roundly beat him last time, the swing voters and moderate Republicans who turned from Trump in 2020 still understand that he hasn't change and has in fact doubled down on all the reasons they voted against him. Nevertheless his polls remain solid, his base of mostly white Christian nationalists has hardly wavered, and tens of millions expected to come out and vote for him in again this year. Mr Trump remains a threat and the charges against him, including new ones outlined in this update, remain timely and relevant.

So back to the start: why does the religious right follow such an obviously immoral man? During an April 2019 interview on a conservative Christian radio show, Minnesota congresswoman, pseudo-spokeswoman for conservative Christian values and human-owl hybrid with the thousand-yard stare, Michelle Bachmann extolled the heavenly credentials of America's 45th, and possibly final president, Donald J. Trump, she claimed, 'is highly biblical, and I would say to your listeners, we will in all likelihood never see a more godly, biblical president again in our lifetime.' If that lifetime is mercifully brief, she may escape the pain of being proven wrong.

As someone who went to Sunday school, this seems a remarkably generous assessment. As I understood it, Christians are supposed to be humble, whereas Mr. Trump is notoriously vainglorious. They must be generous, whereas he is a famous miser. A Christian manages his appetites, yet Trump is a reputed glutton and unrepentant womanizer. A Godly person would surely do his best to honor the Ten Commandments, yet these pages will explain how the president consciously and willfully breaks all of them. Yes, even the one about killing.

Donald Trump seems a curious character for the Christian Right to rally behind. These social conservatives, who make up a large portion of the Republican Party's voter base, have historically prided themselves on their devotion to tradition.

They extol the virtues of faith and fidelity, family values, abstinence, frugality, honesty (of the standard variety; of the intellectual sort I am not so sure), humility, civility, and politeness. Trump, however, has exhibited little interest in religion, has been married several times and committed adultery at least as often; he lives and promotes an ostentatious, gaudy lifestyle, lies with an ease, frequency and blatant transparency rarely seen even in political figures; boasts and brags, goads and bullies and exhibits such public uncouthness that it prompted Republican O.G. Mitt Romney to publicly condemn him for giving speeches 'laced with profanity.' A model Christian, Mr. Trump most certainly is not.

Yet they've flocked to him and stick like flies to the proverbial turd. Nothing Trump does – his affairs, his tax fraud, his bank fraud, his campaign collusion with foreign spies, his incessant and compulsive lying, his disrespect for minorities, women, the disabled, foreign migrants and foreigners in general, not to mention his pandering to white supremacists and other hate organizations – seems to shake the faith of churchgoing Americans in their new orange-faced leader. In fact, Trump received over 80% of the white evangelical vote in 2016 and his support among that base has remained fairly steady. Why do the people of God so adore such an ungodly figure?

Evangelicals are traditionally supporters of Republican candidates for a number of reasons. The party tends to pander to the religious causes of its base and remains a bastion of white

Anglo-Saxon Protestants: Jews, Catholics, and African American churchgoers tend to support the democrats. People do stick with their communities when it comes to voting. The evangelicals have also long been vocal opponents of any form of abortion, so much so they are often labeled single-issue voters: as long as a candidate – again usually Republican – proclaims his (it's usually a he) opposition to abortion and an interest in supporting laws that restrict women's access to the procedure, he can generally count on evangelical support. Mr. Trump has consistently stuck with this boiler-plate Republican position, so it is no surprise they have his back on that one.

But a curious set of other data has come out of the same studies. White evangelicals tend to support hardline immigration policies as well. They are virulently against any form of illegal immigration and have polled unfavorably even toward some legal avenues, such as chain migration, which allows migrants to apply to bring their families over. They oppose many forms of welfare and any notion of a single-payer national healthcare plan, touted these days as Medicare for All. They tend to look unfavorably on Affirmative Action and similar field-leveling policies that give African Americans and other minorities a hand up, believing ostensibly in the notion that a man must pull up his bootstraps and the myth that America truly offers equality for all; so that the disadvantaged shouldn't need a helping hand. They even believe that it is white people and Christians who are the disadvantaged minority in an overly 'politically correct' America beset by secularism, plurality, women's liberation, and multiculturalism.

It should also be noted that white evangelicals are unsurprisingly at their strongest in the deep south and rural states, places that opposed Civil Rights, voting rights and integration, and indeed that at one time attempted to secede from the United States over the right to keep slaves, leading to a bloody civil war. And it is Donald J. Trump who won overwhelmingly in these states. He ran his campaign and in many ways his presidency on racial animus. He began by announcing that illegal immigrants in general are 'rapists,' stoking white male fears about a flood of swarthy Latinos pursuing their women across the border and harking back to the old lynch-mob days when the same charges were leveled at black men. It was Donald Trump who stoked racist anger at his campaign rallies when he demanded a wall be built across the southern border (that Mexico would pay) for, and Trump who exhorted followers to 'knock the hell out of them,' leading in some instances to protesters and detractors – often people of color – being harassed and assaulted at his rallies, live on camera.

Trump also mocked women and the disabled during his campaign. He impugned the religion of a Muslim family whose son, a US Army officer, had died for his country; he demanded a 'complete shutdown of Muslims entering the country,' and referred to the developing nations that migrants and asylum-seekers flee from as 'shithole countries.' It was Donald John Trump who issued the illegal order to his border security services to separate the children of detainees apprehended at the border simply to put the fear into them of trying to enter the country: many of those families have not yet been reunited and some of the children have been abused and died in custody.

Yes, it can be argued that according to the teachings of Christ all life is sacred, or that in the spirit of the Sixth Commandment, broadly speaking abortion is also killing. However, the only time the Bible mentions the act specifically it comes out unequivocally in favor of abortion: the book of Numbers prescribes a forced miscarriage for women suspected of being unfaithful. Even if the evangelical base of Trump ignores that technicality and focuses on the spirit of New Testament teachings, then abortion is maybe the one issue on which they display any modicum of virtue, holding the ostensibly righteous position that everyone including the unborn has the right to life. However, they disregard the contempt that they, Trump and their party display towards the rights of those who have actually been born, including the children of migrants forcibly separated from their families, mistreated and in some cases left to die in government custody. Moreover, the general misanthropy deadly economic disparity, lack of care for the environment and propensity to start wars and bomb civilians are all more or less ignored by those among the Republican base who purport to be the most pious and compassionate.

How could the people of Christ, who fought and died for the downtrodden, who associated with paupers and prostitutes (and not in the way Trump does), washed the feet of the diseased and preached love for one's neighbor and all mankind, possibly find common cause with a leader who openly encourages his followers to do just the opposite? One could be forgiven for coming to the conclusion that the keyword in 'white evangelical' is not 'evangelical'.

So this is the Bible according to Donald Trump: a quasi-religious book by an unreligious author about an irreligious man who has broad religious support. It will again demonstrate through Trump's breach of the Ten Commandments – all of them, and the seven deadly sins just for our Catholic readers – how the president is not only unfit for the support of anyone who calls themselves a Christian, but also how his conduct and demeanor, and snowballing evidence of mental instability, corruption and graft make him unfit for public office in general. According to the Ten Commandments, Mr Trump shouldn't even have been elected Dog Catcher, let alone President. In fact, he should probably be locked up, or if we're to follow the teachings of the Bible, maybe even stoned to death. He most certainly must not be reelected after all the damage he has caused and continues to cause.

1. THOU SHALT WORSHIP NO OTHER GODS BEFORE ME

'Sorry losers and haters, but my I.Q. is one of the highest — and you all know it! Please don't feel so stupid or insecure, it's not your fault.'

- Emoluments, 3:21

The first commandment appears to be the first broken by Trump and his supporters. Trump worships himself above all else, and given the way he talks about himself appears to have more or less deified the imaginary Donald Trump that lives in his head. In order of importance, he also values money, looks up to dictators such as Vladimir Putin and the Saudi Crown Prince, and may even harbor some respect for pathetic inheritor-strongmen such as Kim Jong-Un. He most certainly does not worship God ahead of any of these, if he worships Him all.

First then, himself. Trump loves Trump. He has made no secret of this. Yet this goes beyond mere confidence. According to Donald Trump, the smartest, most educated, most competent and decent human being on the planet is Donald Trump. The most oft-quoted phrase is probably the time when Trump's mental health was publicly questioned and he tweeted the retort that he had gone, 'from very successful businessman to top TV star to President of the United States (on my first try). I think that would qualify as not smart, but genius...and a very stable genius at that!' Of course it was his second try, having pulled out of the 2012 primaries early, but who's counting? Not one so great or stable as Trump. Yet there have been many other instances where Mr. Trump has shown that he trusts nobody's judgment but his own and experts all know less than he does.

When debating his 2016 opponent Hillary Clinton, it was pointed out that Trump had avoided paying taxes for years, to which he replied, 'That makes me smart.' In 2012 when challenging then-President Obama on his country of origin Trump insisted to a CNN host, 'I always told people, you know I'm a very smart guy. I got good marks. I was all this, I went to the best college: the Wharton School of Finance, which to me is like the greatest business school.' Also during the 2016 campaign, he told an MSNBC host, 'I'm speaking with myself, number one, because I have a very good brain and I've said a lot of things...My primary consultant is myself, and I have, you know, I have a good instinct for this stuff.'

After winning the 2016 Republican primary he reminded us, 'I'm not changing. I went to the best schools, I'm, like, a very smart person. I'm going to represent our country with dignity and very well. I don't want to change my personality – it got me here.' Pro tip: if you have to keep saying you're smart, you may not be. But the president's incredible self-belief does not end there: he has questioned experts in almost every field, sometimes even admitting he is working on merely a hunch even as he contradicts those with a lifetime of knowledge. A short roundup is in order:

Trump knows more than scientists. He claimed in 2016, 'I know more about renewables than any human being on Earth.' On Earth he said. This should come as no surprise, because renewables rely on new technology and Trump is also, by his own admission, the world's foremost expert on this as well: 'Nobody knows more about technology than me.' When challenged on his claim that climate change was a hoax perpetrated by China to destroy America's economy, he reminded us that all one needs to understand science is instinct, or perhaps just the right genes: 'My uncle was a great professor at MIT for many years, Dr. John Trump, and I didn't talk to him about this particular subject, but I have a natural instinct for science.' What he makes clear is that one as brilliant as he most certainly need not discuss science with an expert. When he disagreed with the government's own climate report in 2018, Trump had an easy answer for that as well: 'One of the problems that a lot of people like myself − we have very high levels of intelligence, but we're not necessarily such believers.' One only needs to believe, apparently, or not, in order to understand the science of climate change. Or the weather: when a National

Weather Service report contradicted his predicted path for a hurricane, Trump simply drew in a new one with a Sharpie and held up the doctored image on live TV.

Trump is also far wiser than economists. Though he was born to a very wealthy family and has done well with real estate, simply by dint of having inherited enough money to buy some property and watch it increase in value over the years, he believes he has a highly-developed head for business. Despite the fact that his ideas can mostly be condensed into his ghost-written eighties-era book The Art of the Deal, a juvenile treatise that simplifies business transactions into 'winners' and 'losers' and which he appears to have developed after watching Wall Street, his followers generally believe his rags-to-riches cover story and thus are easily fooled when he proclaims himself an expert on monetary matters. He may even believe it himself.

On the economy then, our overweight Gordon Gecko wannabe has plenty to say. When asked about the opinion of the Federal Reserve, Trump soothes us with the quip, 'I think I know about it better than they do.' On finances in general, 'I understand money better than anybody.' Taxes: 'I think nobody knows more about taxes than I do, maybe in the history of the world.' And trade: 'Nobody knows more about trade than me.' His genius did not begin with his presidential campaign: apparently, he has known everything for many years. In 1999, we heard, 'I think nobody knows more about campaign finance than I do, because I'm the biggest contributor.' Clearly, Mr.

Trump knows all there is about all matters economic and financial – just ask him. It feeds nicely into the rightwing assumption that a businessman could run a country, perhaps based on the long held American hero-worship of those who have shown an ability to get rich.

Only Trump has not shown any such ability. He is an incompetent businessman who, despite having been wealthy to begin with, had to be bailed out with family money when his Casinos failed; he has filed for bankruptcy half a dozen times. The only way he has demonstrated an ability to make money is by lying about his wealth to get bank loans and turning that unearned reputation into a name-branding empire. On that, we should perhaps cede him some street smarts, but on the real estate, it does not take a 'stable genius' to buy property and wait for it to appreciate. It only takes money, and he was born with a lot of that. His father left him what in today's term equaled around $400 million. This is a far cry from the 'small loan of a million dollars' he claims to have received from daddy to start his real estate career. It is also a sum that he may have avoided paying inheritance tax on, not because he's 'smart' but because he's a crook. Perhaps the one time he was honest about his business acumen is when he boasted, 'I'm the king of debt. I'm great with debt. Nobody knows debt better than me.'

Yet Trump's apparent genius does not end there. Along with economics and science, he is a self-proclaimed expert on social media, drones, the US visa system, civil engineering projects and curiously, the life and times of New Jersey senator and brief 2020 presidential primary challenger Cory Booker. He also knows a lot about the law, both in terms of the courts and of the government and constitution: 'Who knows more about lawsuits than I do?' Trump challenges us again, 'I'm the king.' This may be true, as he has spent most of his career in and out of court. In the seventies he was sued by the City of New York for discriminating against African American tenants; more recently during his presidential campaign, he agreed to settle a class action suit for $25 million with a group of students defrauded by his dubiously-named Trump University venture. Perhaps because he spends so much time in and out of them, Trump was able to confidently proclaim, 'I know more about courts than any human being on Earth.'

This fine legal acumen may be best demonstrated in his handling of the Mueller Probe, when a special prosecutor was assigned by Congress and the Justice Department to investigate Russian interference into the 2016 election and the level of cooperation the Trump campaign may or may not have provided. His first response was to such rumblings was to fire the head of the FBI James Comey. Failing that he attempted to order the Attorney General to fire the subsequently appointed special prosecutor Robert Mueller. When the Attorney General Jeff Sessions recused himself from the investigation, Trump tried to have him fired, and the deputy Attorney general, and the subsequent head of the FBI, Andrew McCabe. He went on a

Twitter storm for two years decrying the investigation, attempted to fire a bunch of other people involved, threatened to sue or offered to pardon witnesses, instructed other witnesses including his son to give false statements and directed officials not to comply with congressional subpoenas. In other cases when potentially illegal orders to fire this person or that were given, they were quietly ignored. Perhaps Trump forgot to proclaim he has the best memory as well.

Finally when so much obstruction of justice generated calls for impeachment in Congress, the president threatened to go to the Supreme Court, presumably to have any action against him nullified. This is not what the Supreme Court does. It is often touted as 'the highest court in the land' but this is beyond even its powers. Congress represents the people and the people will have the last say. This is what separates a democracy from a dictatorship – or a business – and one can only assume that because he keeps telling us Mr. Trump would be smart enough to know the role of the courts in his presidency.

For such a brilliant legal mind, Trump has shown himself to be woefully unaware of the definition of obstruction of justice, the limits of executive power, the roles of the branches of government and the courts, not to mention the constitutionally prescribed roles and responsibilities of his cabinet members. Unperturbed, this brilliant legal mind called his favorite Fox news host Sean Hannity in late April of 2019 to go on a 45-

minute rant decrying the legal and constitutional challenges against him as an attempted 'coup'.

It might seem bad enough that Trump thinks he knows better than some of the country's most accomplished scientists, economists and legal minds; such things might also be forgivable among his evangelical base, none of who care much for 'pencil necks' anyway and many of which believe the Earth is only a few thousand years old and that humans coexisted with dinosaurs. It's all well and good taking on smarty pants lawyers, politicians and economists, but what of the American Right's beloved military?

The conservatives love them some soldier-boys. They sing prayers at football matches while fighter jets scream overhead; they idolize the military and fly flags on their lawns. They hang around polling stations in camouflage and flags with assault rifles on their shoulders when black people try to vote. Blue collar white America is a large source of recruits for the armed forces. Criticizing any foreign war has been met since the Sixties with the retort that it undermines the troops. The AR-15, beloved automatic rifle of the civilian market and favorite of gun-toting militias, religious cults and synagogue shooters, is a variant of the Army's standard rifle in service for the past 50 years, and most red-blooded Trump supporters can take it apart blindfolded, or at least yap about it for hours.

Trump, in contrast, has had a less than storied military career. In fact, apart from a brief stint at a military boarding school to impose some discipline in his early teens, he has none whatsoever. He has likely never so much as touched a firearm since boarding school and rarely even wears a green tie, though the dead raccoon that serves as his toupee does somewhat hark back to the frontier days of Davy Crockett; or perhaps to the furry headgear worn by Russian soldiers, a far more apt comparison in light of his current allegiances.

During Trump's presidential run it came to light that a young Donald Trump avoided compulsory military service in the sixties, which might have seen him land up in the Vietnam War, by having a doctor proclaim that among other ailments, he suffered from bone spurs in his heel; he does not to this day remember which foot was afflicted. So it might come as a surprise nobody on the Right batted an eyelid when Trump famously claimed not long after his 2015 campaign announcement that he knew more about military matters than the generals.

In this case it was the fight against the Islamic State (ISIS) which had recently taken large swathes of land in Syria and Iraq and was giving the American-led military coalition a run for its money. 'I know more about ISIS than the generals do, believe me,' Trump bluntly put it. He plainly did not. One might argue several years into his presidency and ISIS now militarily defeated, he still doesn't know much about them. But how could a man who has never served in government or the military know more about a military threat than the commanders of the Army,

Navy and Air Force fighting in theater, and the Joint Chiefs of Staff at home? Trump's godlike omniscience does not stop there. He doubled down in the same year during another interview at his second favorite soap-box Fox News, 'There's nobody bigger or better at the military than I am.' In 2016, responding to questions about his fitness to serve as Commander in Chief of the armed forces after his previous statements, he informed us, 'So a general gets on, sent obviously by Obama, and he said, [Trump] knows nothing about defense. I know more about offense and defense than they will ever understand believe me.' When challenged on his plans for America's nuclear arsenal and how to deal with nuclear threats, he assured us, 'There is nobody who understands the horror of nuclear more than me.'

The theme here has been consistent. It is partly just the way Trump talks, but also instructive of the way he thinks. He knows more than everyone, than anyone, than anybody else. Nobody knows as much – or ever has known as much – on a raft of issues he has little to no experience with. Not only does that speak to his state of mind, demonstrating he places himself above all of humanity in intelligence and understanding, but he is asking his followers to do so as well. He wants them to look to him first and foremost in all things, like God, because like God he apparently knows best. This is not a normal condition but then Trump has not led a normal life, not from day one.

Trump believes he is always right because he has never suffered the consequences of being wrong. He has never missed the rent, had a genuine career setback, suffered a financially crippling health scare, or been forced to deal with the devastating end to a dream. He is a man who has mostly always gotten what he wants or gotten away with failures that would pauper the rest of us because we're not rich enough to buy our way out of them: as a wayward youth, it was his father's wealth and connections, not his grades that got him into a good college. When he went bankrupt, the family money was always there to bail him out. When he was caught breaking tenancy laws, he could afford the fines; when sued for defrauding people he could simply pay for their silence in a court settlement and walk away.

In other ways, his self-belief has 'proven' correct. Bluffing his way first to the Republican presidential nomination and then into the White House actually worked. For the first two years of his presidency, he even had a friendly Congress where both houses were held by his party. Though some of his wilder executive orders were overturned by constitutional courts, for the most part, the limits of his authority – real and presumed – remained untested until an opposition-held house confronted him after the November 2018 midterm elections. Many aides and cabinet members have left in disgust, but he has otherwise successfully surrounded himself with sycophants and stooges who confirm his assumptions, at least in his presence.

This enormous confidence in one's own knowledge above all others', as many an armchair psychiatrist may point out, is one of the key indicators of malignant narcissism, a clinical personality disorder. Either that or America is indeed fortunate to have such a polymath in the oval office. But a narcissist or not, the cult leader is not alone. Trump has a following and they are willing to allow this self-worship to fester unabated and unchecked as long as it keeps the opposition party out of power and maintains a modicum of clout disproportionate to their numbers.

Trump's supporters are equally sacrilegious, in this case worshipping the great Orange Orator above God, even their twisted version of Him. The fervor with which he is defended even amidst all the evidence of wrongdoing is flabbergasting. If he commits adultery, apparently the Christian Right and so-called conservatives are willing to give him a pass. If he attempts to collude with foreign agents to unseat a hated political opponent, at least it's all for a good cause. If he cheats the people and the government by using his own office for personal gain, he is just a 'smart businessman'. In their eyes, Trump can do no wrong and any attempt to point out Trump's failings results in a vociferous personal attack on the observer for daring to challenge the wisdom of their new deity. They wear his paraphernalia at packed rallies (over their camouflage of course), chant his name like a gospel song and defend his every transgression with grim determination. This can only be explained as a cult of personality.

When Trump claims to be 'smart' his supporters can easily lap that one up. It's the proverbial low-hanging fruit of a sort. One can always point to his business successes – deceptive as they are – and the fact that he won an election against the odds, and say that it demonstrates a certain intelligence. It could be some of that, or it could simply point to a certain shrewdness, or the shameless will to say and do literally anything to win, which in turn leads to the question of how credulous his audience must be and what he truly thinks of them. Is he that sharp or are they just easily fooled? Is he a strategic genius or just a more efficient conman? Historians can have a crack at that one in the future.

We also know that at Trump's Mar-A-Lago retreat in Florida, as well as other resorts and golf clubs he owns, there was a framed picture on the wall of his 2009 TIME Magazine cover. The catch? TIME had never released such a cover. It was created by an artist commissioned by Trump and existed only in his imagination, yet he happily showcased it to visitors. He finally did get on the cover of TIME after winning the 2016 presidential election, as every president-elect does, in his case along with the unflattering tagline, President of the Divided States of America. Trump called the headline 'snarky.' His son later complained of not getting a second cover in 2019.

Even after Trump's humiliating 2020 loss to Joe Biden, the former president continued to aggrandize himself. If the pre-election scenes of Republicans bowing to cheesy gilded statues in the likeness of Trump weren't bad enough (see next chapter), Trump went on to create a new litany of honors for himself. At his own resort's tournament Trump proclaimed in 2024, 'It is my great honor to be at Trump International Golf Club in West Palm Beach tonight, AWARDS NIGHT, to receive THE CLUB CHAMPIONSHIP TROPHY & THE SENIOR CLUB CHAMPIONSHIP TROPHY,' the 77-year-old Trump wrote, adding, 'I WON BOTH!'

Not content with granting himself trophies at his own golf resorts, Trump happily proclaimed himself another award out of thin air, on the spot. In a campaign stop in Detroit he announced, 'You know, I got the 'Man of the Year' in Michigan. Years ago, long before politics, like 12, 13 years ago.' This is apparently a repeat of an old lie told several years before. Exactly what body – the state, the governor, a newspaper, magazine or some business association awarded this prize is never mentioned. He was in Michigan and apparently he was once given an award. CNN's fact checkers stated, **Trump's claim remains false. Nobody has ever been able to find any evidence that he was ever named 'Man of the Year' in Michigan before he ran for president. The state itself does not give out a 'Man of the Year' award; Trump has never lived in Michigan; and he has never specified who supposedly gave him this award and when.'**

Followers may be quite willing to allow themselves to believe Trump is 'right', on climate change, on science, on the economy, and in business because he tells them what they've always wanted to hear. They will permit his vainglorious golfing 'trophies' and fake TIME covers and imaginary Man of the Year proclamations. Those who claim God chose him for one reason or another – to stamp out abortion, restore conservative judges to the courts, put religion back in schools or just 'save' Christmas from the Muslims and liberals, are deifying him in their own way. Trump may even be beginning to believe the praise. When conservative radio host Wayne Allyn Root extolled Trump's support of Israeli Prime Minister Netanyahu's hardline government and claimed 'Israelis love him like he's the second coming of God,' the president happily and predictably retweeted the comments.

It is, of course, all a sham and part of the long con. As his party applauds fiscal conservatism and monetary discipline, Trump's history of business failures speaks of extravagance and waste – a waste he has brought to government: Forbes magazine estimates Trump had blown over $100 million on golf trips alone by the middle of his first term even as the national deficit ballooned to over a trillion. Evangelicals maintain staunch support for 'family values' while Trump's affairs and alleged sexual assaults suggest he has precious few. Likewise, on the military, Republican hypocrisy once again rears its ugly head. Conservatives, the right-wing, evangelicals and Republican voters all make a point of revering the armed forces, which makes it perplexing they should accept Trump's vilification of generals who correct him and his claims to know better than the experts. They purport to stand for the truth while overlooking, accepting, promoting and gladly disseminating his lies. They claim he is the second coming and he is happy to accept it. And from Trump's own pantheon of worship, he has given them new false idols to adore alongside him.

2. THOU SHALT NOT BOW TO ANY GRAVEN IMAGE

'Not all of those people were neo-Nazis, believe me. Not all of those people were white supremacists by any stretch. There were very fine people on both sides.'

- Corruptions, 5:12

Donald Trump hasn't actually carved an image of an ox or an eagle and prayed to it, but he has come about as close as any President of the United States to date. Not only does he worship himself and love to see his name in lights – on hotels, apartment blocks, casinos, and also apparently packaged meat – he also has his own line of cheap hats and ties. If nothing else he knows how to make a buck off his name. But more than this he has also bowed down to the statues of those who betrayed their country and sought to enslave others and he has held up that most false of idols, the beloved firearm, in order to curry favor with the gun lobby and its own sub-cult. With these tools, Trump seeks to further build a mythology and a personality cult around him that demands the blind worship of his followers, even in the face of facts that expose him as a fraud.

The first and biggest of Trump's idols must surely be himself. Just as he worships himself like a god; he seems to enjoy his fat orange face or his silly-sounding name plastered over all manner of edifices. Like all rich bastards, he also likes to commission pictures of himself, for which apparently few other buyers can be found. One can imagine when he sits on the West Wing crapper at four in the morning, tweeting madly away at Meryl Streep, Arnold Schwarzenegger or whichever celebrity he feels most recently slighted by, he does so facing a sizeable portrait of himself on the back of the door. Trump owns several such paintings, acquired of course, through ill-gotten gains. He cannot help it.

Once upon a time, there was a lonely rich man named Donald. He wanted to set up a charity, as many rich people do, to attach some goodwill to his name and to be known for something more than just being born filthy rich. Fibbing about his 'rags to riches' success was not merely enough so the Trump Foundation was born. Though it occasionally did collect and distribute money for worthy causes, it was mostly used as a slush fund and a laundering scheme for Trump to pay himself. Founded in 1988, the foundation was quickly put to work settling all manner of Trump's accounts leading to a slew of legal challenges and the foundation's eventual dissolution and forced closure by the state of New York, while he sat in office as 45th President of the United States. This one bears repeating. The President of the United States had his own charity shut down due to corruption.

How much corruption? Though it was broadly closed under 'Failure to maintain proper governance', there is a long list of offenses that come under that heading: soliciting donations without a license, coordinating foundation grants with his own presidential campaign and using Trump Foundation money to settle Trump Organization legal disputes; donating Foundation money to other politician's campaigns, diverting business or personal income to the foundation as untaxed donations, granting money to charities that rented Trump Organization facilities, and making grants to other private foundations without fulfilling IRS 'expenditure responsibility' rules. The foundation also promised to donate money to various causes such as veteran's groups and 9/11 victims and failed to make those donations, paying only later when Trump was reminded to do so. In several particularly egregious cases, Trump used foundation money to buy stuff he merely wanted. These included football star Tim Tebow's helmet, luxury trips overseas, and reaping profits from charity events held at his resorts, possibly violating IRS self-dealing rules.

Most relevant to the Second Commandment however was charity diverted towards idolatry. Not once but three times, Trump used foundation money to purchase portraits of himself at auctions that were meant to raise money for a foundation cause:

in 2007 he snapped up one fetching six-foot head and shoulders for a bargain $20,000 – using foundation money, not his own. It was followed in 2014 by another $20,000 offering at a Children's charity: at only four feet for the same price this demonstrated that in the highly competitive market for Trump portraits, their value was rising. However, the cake was taken in the intervening years with the help of a straw purchaser, when Trump acquired a $60,000 spread standing at nine feet tall. This may be the one in his bathroom providing stern overwatch to his poop-tweets. These were all bought with Foundation money earmarked for charity causes, some of it from outside donors. Not only was the practice rather cheap, it perhaps reflected his understanding of the true value of the 'artwork' he bought: it wasn't worth spending his own money on.

In addition to his various portraiture and hard-won magazine covers, Trump has also made a habit of adorning his various properties, and those of others, with his own name, preferably in gold leaf. Trump Towers, Trump Place and the Trump International Hotel; Trump Palace and Trump Royale, Trump Park Avenue and the comparatively modest Trump Building: one gets the feeling if he'd been poor, he'd have been an inveterate tagger, such is his obsession with seeing his name plastered on everything in sight. Like a small dog lifting its leg to reach higher up the pole, you'll find the giant letters TRUMP emblazoned on hotels, resorts, apartment blocks and other facilities around the world. There's the trademark tower in

Manhattan where his campaign attempted to conspire with foreign agents to influence the 2016 election; Vegas hotels where he walked in on teen beauty contestants in their changing rooms; and the erstwhile planned tallest-building-in-Moscow that marred his dealings during the 2016 campaign and beyond with claims of having compromising business contacts with Russian developers. Trump loves to slap his name on things even when he should be more discreet.

Not all of these buildings are owned by Trump; in some cases, he licenses his name to other developers for the rights, but its stock has declined recently and the name is less in demand in many circles since his presidential campaign and victory. Though he has made good coin out of the real estate (who would have known property would appreciate?), Trump's further attempts at branding have seen the ill-fated Trump Casinos, Trump Airlines and packaged meat in the form of Trump Steaks. Dedicated carnivores and frequent flyers will be pleased to know they needn't actually buy into a piece of The Donald to get their fix, as none of these ventures got off the ground.

Nevertheless, Trump Organization branding patents still exist in China and the Middle East among other places. These have raised more allegations of self-dealing or breaking the 'Emoluments Clause' of the Constitution, which forbids a sitting president from profiting from his office or receiving gifts or titles from a foreign government. It is safe to say a knighthood from the Queen is not pending as of the time of writing.

In addition to slapping his name on all manner of property, Trump has also published a handful of books over the years, all ghost-written and all showing him in a favorable light. These perhaps are the true Trump Bibles: groveling plaudits that are part memoir, part self-help but mostly total bullshit. We know this because the people who actually wrote the books have come out and told us.

The crown jewel in this stack of low-grade toilet paper is 1987's *The Art of the Deal*, ghostwritten by columnist Tony Schwartz. One magazine called the book, 'a boastful, boyishly disarming, thoroughly engaging personal history'. Its author called it 'putting lipstick on a pig,' and later, 'the biggest regret of my life.' The book certainly captures the spirit of the eighties where a megalomaniac businessman dishes out the sort of recycled 'go get 'em' mantras that the iconic 1980s film Wall Street was famous for. What is remarkable is right when the so-called real estate mogul was publishing this treatise on how to get rich in the booming Manhattan eighties, his businesses were failing spectacularly.

Tax receipts and financial records released in 2019 showed that between 1985 and 1994 Donald J. Trump did not make a dime. In fact over a decade or so, he lost 1.17 billion dollars. This is not a typo. Donald Trump lost a billion dollars. He lost so much and so often (his failed airline, casinos, Trump steaks) that all he was left with was real estate, which anyone born rich could afford to buy and hold onto anyway. Every time he tried an actual business venture it went belly up. He lost so much money he convinced the IRS he didn't even have to pay tax for eight years, which he boasted in a 2016 presidential debate was because he's 'smart'. While Trump was playing Gordon Gecko in his mind and his books, he was achieving nothing of the sort himself in his real business – a curious exercise in life imitating art imitating life.

It also came out in 2019 court filings and the confessions of his arrested and convicted personal lawyer Michael Cohen that Trump's 'secret' to success was simply lying. His organization inflated the value of assets in order to secure loans, later deflating those same assets to pay lower property taxes. Trump then claimed losses to avoid tax altogether and in some cases even listed the losses of his investors as his own in order to pay even less tax. None of this brilliant 'business acumen' seems to have made it into *The Art of the Deal*, yet failure was no deterrent to this billion-dollar loser publishing a book on success. Like all tyrants and cult-leaders, he knows at least how to market himself and in a rare business victory, the book sold well.

Other books published in Trump's name include 1990's *Surviving at the Top*, also written during the height of his losing streak, the *Art of the Comeback*, an unintentionally honest title from 1997; The America we Deserve in 2000; the ironically named *How to Get Rich* in 2004, *Think Like a Billionaire, The Way to the Top, Never Give Up* and a host of other self-help coffee-table rags that carry his name but none of his content.

Never a prolific reader, and far too busy promoting himself to write more than a 140-character tweet, all were written by paid hacks like Schwartz, some more repentant than others.

Unsolicited sycophants are also welcome at the altar. Newspaper mogul, Canadian citizen and convicted fraudster Conrad Black served four years in prison and was deported, barred from entering the US for thirty years. For a man in his late sixties, this amounted to 'for life'. Yet in 2018, Mr. Black wrote the glowing propaganda piece, *Donald J Trump: A President Like No Other*. For this fine tome, Black received a full presidential pardon in 2019, his criminal convictions expunged. Was there really any other way to impress the Idolater-in-Chief than to carve yet another graven image? For praying at his altar, or better yet, building him a new one, President Trump will make all your sins disappear.

And build a new one they did. At the 2021 Conservative political Action Conference, a gold leaf statue of Trump was unveiled. This cartoonish figure had the same outlandish hair, was generously thinner, wore a suit jacket and red tie and stars-and-stripes shorts while holding the front page of the constitution. It would have made for a decent novelty if not for the legion of supplicants who lined up to kiss, fondle and pray over it. This messianic imagery most surely violates the commandment against graven images.

Unfortunately, the Cult of Trump shares much of its iconography with other sinister groups, which the 45th president has done a fine job of co-opting since his run. Quick to seize on the sentiments of the far-right, Donald Trump can be seen and heard, hugging and caressing the US flag in a rather creepy manner, praising the monuments to slave-owning civil war 'heroes' such as General Robert E. Lee and promoting that most American of cultural icons, the good old-fashioned firearm.

At several rallies, as both candidate and president, Trump seems to have gotten overly fresh with pieces of cloth. Just as he boasted once (or more) of groping women without their consent, his wandering hands are quick to cop a feel of the Stars and Stripes. It was a curious sight, watching as what one reporter called 'a mentally unwell old man' sauntered across the stage, to where an American flag hung from its pole in limp resignation, wrapped his arms around it, pressed his cheek to the fabric and offered up an enormous, shit-eating grin to a cheering audience. On one occasion he appeared to stroke the material lovingly, pretending that perhaps it was one of his mistresses. It is often speculated these days he gets little affection from his wife.

Patriotism aside, a flag is just a symbol of a nation, not the nation itself. While it is admirable to show some respect for it, the Bible explicitly states it is not a duty. The Catholic and Orthodox churches split in the middle ages over the use of icons. Despite Trump's inadvertent acknowledgment that many of his followers have indeed reduced the flag to fetishism and were quite willing to play along when he exhibited the same tendencies, a well-meaning patriot might be able to insist that in their love of 'God and Country,' God still comes first. Yeah, whatever helps them sleep at night.

But the right-wing cult's blind worship of the flag, without apparently subscribing to the values of equality and justice it is supposed to represent, is not limited to the flag of the United States of America. The famous 'Stars and Bars' of the southern confederacy, that rebelled against the United States and eventually lost the civil war, also seems to hold a special place in their hearts and has found its way into Trump's rallies. This flag at least makes no such bold claims for the betterment of humanity. It stands instead for segregation and slavery, the dominion of one race over another; an idea perhaps closer to the hearts of most Trump supporters. And here also we see their worship – and his – of that vilest of icons, a statue to another deity.

Robert E. Lee was by most reliable accounts, a total prick. He owned slaves, he bought and sold and traded them; he beat and tortured them when they tried to flee or disobeyed him; he separated slave families in a chilling premonition of the Trump administration's 2018 policy regarding migrants and asylum-seekers at the southern border. Though asked by President Lincoln to lead the Union Army, he instead marched rebel forces against the United States government because it tried to prevent him from doing all these things. This rank traitor eventually lost his war and rather than being imprisoned, exiled or executed, was magnanimously sent home to live out his days in relative luxury despite the inconvenience of no longer being able to own other human beings. This is not a man that any American patriot owes any respect.

One night in Charlottesville Virginia in 2017, a group of fairly clean-cut neatly dressed young white men with mildly fascist hairdos marched through the city streets holding blazing Tiki torches and chanting, 'The Jews will not replace us.' They had come from around the country to protest the proposed removal of a statue of General Lee from a city park, though it is not clear how many of Charlottesville's tiny Jewish population were responsible for this measure. This rally lasted several days and not everyone looked as photogenic as the J.C. Penny white boys in button-down shirts, though they were at least as hateful: it included a mix of skinheads, bikers, the usual camouflage- and flackjacket-clad militia members; bearded Aryan Brotherhood types looking like the best Wagner stage extras, carrying not only the confederate flag, but swastikas and symbols from other white supremacist groups; red 'make America Great Again' hats from the Trump rallies and campaign merchandisers, and no small number of weapons including firearms.

Though there was little chance of these fine fellows being 'replaced' by the Jews – a minority in the United States that makes up a whopping two percent – their graven images to the false gods of the failed Confederacy were indeed under threat.

This was not only just as God had commanded several thousand years ago, but updated by local and state legislatures due to more modern concerns: in the wake of a shooting at a black church in Charleston, South Carolina, an attack of national conscience ensured such hate-inspiring confederate monuments were being removed across the country. Statues to southern insurgents and turncoats such as Jefferson Davis and the aforementioned Robert E. Lee, who did indeed cut a fine figure on horseback in this particular representation, were finally being removed after a century (or in some case just a couple of decades) much to the chagrin of the supporters who idolized them.

The white tide was met by counter-protesters, most notably the militant Antifa (Anti-fascist) group, but also various peace movements, women's organizations, student unions and church congregations. Naturally such a confrontation led to violence which President Trump only half-heartedly condemned, noting there were 'Good people on both sides'. This was a lie. There were no 'good people' on the right: they had come to spread hate and division, even those who did not take part in the violence. After street battles where one black man was beaten viciously on camera, another was almost shot, and dozens of 'good people on both sides' were arrested, the riot culminated in an act of domestic terrorism, wherein a right-wing sympathizer drove a vehicle at speed into a crowd of peaceful marchers, killing one and injuring others. The president was silent about this tragedy for two days after before releasing a belated condemnation, with a wink and a nod to people he knew damn well were his supporters.

Though the Charlottesville killer was dragged into court, Trump was undeterred in his worship of radicals such as General Lee. In October of 2018 and again in early 2019, the president used the pulpit at rallies to praise the good general. When challenged on his earlier Charlottesville comments Trump explained, 'I was talking about people that went because they felt very strongly about the monument to Robert E. Lee, a great general. Whether you like it or not, he was one of the great generals.' Except he lost, and Trump is supposed to hate losers. As a man who used spurious medical grounds to avoid military service in his own youth, Trump can hardly be expected to take a sudden interest in martial matters in his old age. Instead, he was pandering to these supporters of the Antebellum South and giving them another not-so-subtle 'hint' that he supports their white supremacist sympathies. And to that end, the furor over the removal of statues remains, with president Trump firmly on the side of those who wish to continue bowing down at the altar of traitorous 'heroes' of a bygone age. He cynically exploits this return to some form of pseudo-animist ancestor worship that the likes of Abraham and Moses once sought to do away with.

But when he is not in the Deep South or at a Klan rally, Trump must return to the patriotic symbolism of now and the good old Stars and Stripes. America has grown steadily more patriotic over the years since September 11, at least in terms of symbolism. College and professional football games, in particular, have turned into pseudo-nationalist rallies of a sort, with military parades, recruiting stalls, Air Force flyovers, and players and spectators all standing for the flag and the national anthem before the match. Well, not all of them.

When the American pastime of police shooting young unarmed black men spiked up in the mid-2010s, it spawned all manner of protests and action groups. Chief among these was Black Lives Matter, a loose coalition of church groups, parents and civic organizations that marched in many cities to protest the violence. Their message was simple: that too many black men were either killed on the spot or died in custody and the relevant police departments were not doing enough to investigate the deaths of reign in over-zealous officers. Naturally, Fox News denounced the marchers as anti-American militants.

In solidarity, two organizations with a prominent number of high profile African-Americans saw a chance to add to these voices. The NFL and the NBA have a long and storied history of giving young black men opportunity and a few standouts, already known for giving back to the community, saw the chance to lend their names to a cause they believed in. One of the earliest and most notable athletes to take a stand – or a knee in this case – was Colin Kapernick of the San Francisco 49ers. At several matches, when everyone else was standing during the Star-Spangled Banner, hands on hearts and chins aloft, Kapernick kneeled in solidarity with those who had yet to experience social justice under the ideals set out in the constitution of the republic, as represented by that very flag and anthem. He was admonished; his own contract was not renewed after the season but his protest caught on and soon whole teams were doing it, both in football and basketball.

The Christian Right, of course, exploded. Raised to worship an America that had always been much more protective of their rights, white conservatives and their media mouthpieces roundly condemned the mostly African-American protestors. They were decried as unpatriotic and un-American, sacrilegious. Trump was right there to defend his beloved icon as well. While team owners were threatening to fine players who did not stand for the anthem and Fox News was having a field day of faux-patriotism, the president weighed in during his own speeches and early-morning tweets from the presidential toilet stall.

All through the spring and summer of 2018, his tiny orange thumbs and big loud mouth worked furiously to condemn those who lent their voices to the voiceless. 'You're proud of our country, you're proud of our history, and unlike the NFL, you always honor and cherish our great American flag,' he told another rally audience of white faces in red hats. He went on that year to muse, 'Why is the NFL getting massive tax breaks while at the same time disrespecting our Anthem, Flag and Country?' With this cry to the heavens unanswered, Trump fumed, 'If the players stood proudly for our Flag and Anthem, and it is all shown on broadcast, maybe ratings could come back?' When the ratings did not change he decided to inject more politics: 'I asked [Vice President Mike] Pence to leave the stadium if any players kneeled, disrespecting our country. I am proud of him.' Pence did leave the stadium once, in a grandly-staged act and at taxpayer expense for showing up to a game he had never intended to sit through. In the end, when Kapernick's movement outlasted the dreaded orange tweets, Trump fell back to his default position on people of color: those who protested he suggests, 'Maybe shouldn't be in the country.'

By midseason, the whole league was defiant, with many white players now kneeling or at least courageously staying in the locker during the anthem in solidarity with their black teammates. Instead of welcoming the winning Philadelphia Eagles to the White House, who had pointedly refused the president's traditional invitation, Trump was forced to hold a ceremony to 'celebrate America' where the flag was raised and the anthem played. In all tweeting several dozen times and commenting all most as often at speeches and rallies, Trump managed to rile up his base into a foaming hatred of any 'colored' person who dare to defy the Stars and Stripes. The final message was clear: forget the ideals the country was founded on and bow down blindly to its symbols instead. Two men were still seen taking a knee on the White House lawn.

Trump has put up his own name, the flag of the country and worse the flags and statues of its traitors as idols to be worshipped. The book of Exodus was clear on this matter – it's a big no-no. While modern Christians may argue it was specifically a rule for the Hebrews under Moses, or that a certain amount of idolatry is permitted since the medieval split of the Eastern and Western churches, this devotion to idols other than God's own seems like hypocritical impiety at best. Perhaps like so many things done in the name of the Lord, this commandment is just a convenient stick to beat other religions with. But that raises the question of what really is the best use for things done in the Lord's name, and to what purpose should the name of God itself be used?

3.   THOU SHALT NOT TAKE THE NAME OF THE LORD IN VAIN.

'Two Corinthians 3:17, that's the whole ballgame…is that the one you like?'

\- Vanities, 4:12

Viewers who tuned in to Donald Trump's social media site around Easter of 2024 might have been mildly bemused (even amused) to see the former President on video, promoting his latest book. On the other hand, by this stage in his long career of grifting, nothing should have come as a surprise. Beset with multiple court battles and spiraling legal costs, his team had been fumbling about for ways to raise cash. There were appeals on the websites Kickstarter and GoFundMe, sales of Trump-branded non-fungible tokens – cute online digital stamps that were elsewhere selling for millions among art collectors and celebrities – and even gaudy gold sneakers.

But this time it was something not unique or new at all. In fact, one may wonder what took Trump so long to latch onto it. This time he was selling something that could be bought for pennies at opportunity shops and second-hand stores, read for free online or in any hotel bedroom (see Chapter Seven for more on how Trump spends his time in those), and handed out for free at church. Most homes where his supporters dwell already have at least one copy in any case. The Donald was reduced to pimping the Holy Bible.

This wasn't any Bible however. This one was endorsed by Donald Trump, signed by him and came with two other vital and several other largely free-to-read documents including the Bill of Rights and the United States Constitution. Said Trump, 'Religion and Christianity are the biggest things missing from this country, and I truly believe that we need to bring them back and we have to bring them back fast.' These weren't the only things missing however. Conspicuously absent from Trump's version of the constitution are amendments 11-27 – those covering inconvenient clauses such as the abolition of slavery, granting the right to vote to women and people of color, the Electoral College, presidential term limits and the insurrection clause (see Chapters Six and nine). All this free literature, minus the missing bits of course, could be bought online for the bargain price of $59.99.

Trump cut a pathetic figure as he mumbled dispassionately through the teleprompter. He looked sheepish and deflated, as though he finally realized how low he'd finally sunk. Of all the failed attempts to make money for his 2024 campaign, to pay off his legal expenses or just fleece the faithful for a few more dollars and one more time, this was surely his most pathetic. 'All Americans need a Bible in their home and I have…many,' Mr

Trump assured us. 'It's my favorite book. It's many people's favorite book.'

The third commandment can be cryptic. To 'take something in vain' is not an expression commonly used in modern English. It is widely interpreted as simply not using 'God' or 'Christ' as expletives. Yet it more importantly encompasses making promises before God or in God's name that you will not keep, or disingenuously swearing on the Bible, by Christ, Mary, God or the Holy Ghost in order to demonstrate false piety. Put more succinctly, one should not invoke the Lord's name in a trivial manner. We should perhaps add to this Christ's comments on cursing in general, including, 'Let no unwholesome word proceed from your mouth.' Trump must have heard him and said, 'Hold my beer.'

The 45th president is by no means the first to make a habit of cussing, but he may be the most prolific. Nixon dropped the odd F-bomb in the darkest days of his Watergate troubles, but for the most part, Republican presidents are pretty pious when it comes to their language: they've had to be in order to court the churchgoers. But apparently, Trump is allowed to throw that playbook out the window. Republican old-guarder Mitt Romney condemned him early in his primary campaign for among other things, giving speeches 'laced with profanity.' Trump proceeded to pass another beer and double down.

The list of Trump speech profanities, to put it mildly, is long and storied. Dozens of speeches have contained filth, insults, taunts and jabs that would make any Midwestern pastor's wife blush. Bear in mind these same hypocritical cunts voted for him en masse so perhaps we needn't be so concerned with what they'd find offensive. They will likely vote for Trump again. But that does not mean they wouldn't blush. Partly to hone the image of a straight-shooter, Trump makes a point of sounding politically incorrect. Let us look at some of his stand-out rants from both the campaign and rallies held after taking office:

In response to the take-a-knee protestors – the athletes who refused to stand for the anthem before football and basketball games in protest against police violence against the African American community – he was equally blunt. Trump said of football player Colin Kapernick, 'Get that son of a bitch off the field.' Of potential terrorists – or perhaps any Muslim he sets his sights on: 'I would bomb the shit out of them.' Primary opponent Ted cruise was a 'pussy'. This may have been a correct assessment as the Texas Congressman became a supporter after losing to Trump; less so his boast in a famous leaked tape that it was okay to grab women 'by the pussy' because he was famous, and childishly mimicked the way a disabled reporter walked and talked in a juvenile display at one of his rallies that was filmed live on TV. We should perhaps be thankful he showed more restraint during his inaugural address. These are but the tip of the iceberg because four-letter words all too frequently constantly crop up in Trump's speeches.

Despite being merely foul-mouthed, frowned upon as it is, Trump deserves special citation for being Biblically as blasphemous as possible when it comes to the Lord's name. In this he as shown little equal, regardless of the fact that he is the darling of the most militantly Christian voting bloc in the country. This not to say he can be heard hollering about Jesus H. Christ left and right because on that count his parents seem to have raised him well enough. It is rather because he appropriates the name of God for his own purposes. The occasional curse using God's name as an epithet may be the most common form of blasphemy and the most obvious. However religious scholars will explain that taking the name in vain specifically refers to falsely swearing oaths, disingenuously praying or otherwise pretending to invoke God's favor without meaning it at all. This is the most insidious and dangerous form of breaking the third commandment: gaining a free ride on God's coattails. In claiming to be doing God's work and standing up for His believers, Trump is conning them in the name of the Lord. In many a speech, he has referred to America as a Christian nation, joined the outcry against the alleged 'War on Christmas' often bemoaned in right-wing circles, and waxed on about the sanctity of the unborn. These are unlikely to be because he holds such values, but he knows his supporters do. For these reasons, evangelical leaders have flocked to Trump's banner, bringing whole congregations with them like cultists to the Kool-Aid fountain.

Mr. Trump cannot be unaware of what he's doing when he hams it up for this audience. Feeding off a roomful of cheers, he knows how to get a crowd on its feet. In one speech alone at dead grifter Jerry Falwell's disingenuously named evangelical brainwashing center, Liberty College in 2017, Trump went on a binge of co-opted religious symbolism. He called America a nation of 'True believers,' And on the subject of whether heaven helped his election win, recalled hearing his campaign, 'would require major help from God…and we got it.' 'Have pride in your beliefs,' he further advised graduates, and 'Be a warrior for the truth,' fighting for 'God's precious gift of freedom.' This comes from the mouth of a president who has advised shutting down news agencies that criticize him and locking up his political opponents; who praises dictators such as Russia's Putin and North Korea's Kim Jong-Un. On the late Founder of the university, known for his avid support of segregationists, Apartheid, homophobia, Islamophobia and stinking great bags of freshly printed cash, Trump said, 'Reverend Falwell's life is a testament to the power of faith to change the world.'

This comes from the mouth of a boorish fat man who the conservatives love but their values utterly disdain. They demand fidelity, monogamy and chastity: Trump has cheated on all three of his wives. They expect presidential piety but he has never been a churchgoing man; they preach charity yet his own foundation seems to have been used for money laundering at best and appears to have hoarded more than it ever gave away; they recommend moderation but he eats a bucket of chicken for breakfast. Most of all however, the Christian Right surely expects someone to be sincere in their beliefs, yet much in the way he uses the flag, Donald Trump deploys religion as a mere prop. In case the stakes weren't high enough, he reminded another of his audiences that they may next lose the name of God altogether if they don't fight for it: 'People are so proud to be using that beautiful word, God. And they are using the word God again and they are not hiding from it. And they are not being told to take it down. And they are not saying we cannot honor God. In God We Trust, so important,'

It is no surprise that religion makes for such an easy sloganeering. American Christians, quite unlike their European counterparts seem to have the idea they are someone special; the chosen few who escaped religious persecution to found a new Christian nation – their manifest destiny. It is indeed to them, one nation under God – their god to be precise; therefore a nation under them, really. To them it is a nation founded on white identity: the supremacy over African slaves was supported by religious excuses and biblical verse; the Native Americans were mere heathens to be cleared from the new 'promised land' the way Abraham smote the Philistines, or something. The founding pilgrims have long been cast as religious refugees; in fact, the pilgrims were too strict in their beliefs and wanted to be free to persecute and exclude on their own terms, hence the necessity to sail halfway around the world, massacre the local inhabitants and start over. In that sentiment, by pretending to stand for their religious values, Trump finds the opportunity to exploit credulity and pretend to be doing God's work.

This religious commitment to a racial hierarchy was put on display in the summer of 2020, as race-related protests raged across the country. Following yet another police killing of yet another unarmed black man in Minnesota, the Black Lives Matter (BLM for short) was spawned from a loose confederacy of advocates' groups, churches and the Antifa movement. Some of the protests against police violence got out of hand and there were cases of looting and property damage. When the street protests reached Washington DC, President Trump spent some time hunkered in a White House bunker, mulling whether he could legally send the Army out to clear the streets.

The president had consistently dismissed the complaints of the BLM movement over the previous weeks and had even stated, 'When the looting starts, the shooting starts.' On June 1, Trump met with Attorney general Bill Barr and Joint Chiefs Chairman Gen. Mark Milley to discuss using the insurrection act to deploy US soldiers to 'Just shoot them in the legs or something.' They demurred, and was eventually handled by law enforcement, Trump took the opportunity to march to the well-known St John's Episcopal Church, which had been partly damaged in the protests, for a photo-op. With police tear-gassers dispersing crowds and an entourage of bodyguards, cabinet members and Gen. Milley in tow, Trump arrived on the Church's front lawn to pose for the cameras. His daughter Ivanka furnished him with a bible, which he held *upside down* in a ham-fisted attempt to marry up his religious pretensions with his authoritarian instincts and remind people of color who was in charge and by Whose command.

June First was just the latest attempt of the right to co-opt Christianity into their culture wars. Switch on Fox News just around the start of the holiday season every year (or any network owned by the right-wing Murdochs or the kindred Sinclair Media Group) and you'll hear about how the traditional Christian values of America are being eroded through an insidious 'War on Christmas.' The narrative is simple and rather full of holes, but a good sell to true believers. Starting around the time the godless heathen Kenyan pretender Barack Obama seized a presidency reserved for White Anglo-Saxon Protestants, the trend of department stores and greeting cards offering a more inclusive 'Happy Holidays' over the traditional 'Merry Christmas' began to gather pace. Depending on whom you ask, this could have been seen as a mere welcome to all faiths and creeds in a multi-ethnic society to share in the festive season, or a symptom of creeping Sharia Law. Fox host Sean Hannity chose the latter, as did anyone else trying to push the narrative that Obama is a closet Muslim looking to hand the country over to the Taliban. As mentioned, the fewer questions one asks, the easier this narrative is to swallow.

As this story has been popular on the right, dutifully resurrected every holiday season…sorry Christmas season, it makes for a handy narrative to be appropriated by a right-wing presidential candidate eager to display his credentials to a 'persecuted' Christian base apparently in imminent danger of once again being rounded up and fed to the lions, or at least getting a visit from the Grinch. In 2016 during his run for office, Trump made sure to tackle this important issue during an interview: 'You know, you go from one thing to the next to the point where it's not politically correct to say 'Merry Christmas' to anybody, or you go to stores and you don't ever see the word 'Christmas' anymore,' said the candidate. 'We are going to start saying 'Merry Christmas' again.'

As if to make sure we are tracking his progress, Trump reminded us a year into his presidency, amid disputes with allies, tensions with Iran, swirling rumors that he colluded with Russian agents and a hot war in Syria and Iraq with the Islamic State, that he really did have a handle on the most pressing needs of the day: 'When I first started campaigning, people were not allowed, or in some cases foolishly ashamed, to be using in stores Merry Christmas, Happy Christmas. They would say Happy Holidays, you would never see Christmas.' Thankfully as of 2018, the battle appeared to have been won. Trump proudly declared to a rally in mid-July, 'Remember the attack on Merry Christmas? They're not attacking it anymore. Everyone's happy to say Merry Christmas, right? Merry Christmas! That was under siege.

You'd have these big department stores that say, happy holidays. They say where's the Merry Christmas? Now they're all putting up Merry Christmas again. And that's because only because of our campaign.'

In short, Trump picked a fight that didn't exist then declared he won it. He'll do it again next year, no doubt, a perpetual War on Christmas, fought every year, now with the added bonus of a renewable Trump victory in the short, addled memory of his base. Fool me once.

Yet nowhere is Trump's disingenuous piety more openly on display than his sudden support for anti-abortionists. Trump had been a socially liberal New Yorker and a supporter of the democrats before suddenly switching parties in the years just before his first political project: slandering Barack Obama as an alleged foreigner with a fake birth certificate. By then Trump had realized that if he were to ever run for office he would do so as a Republican. Not because his values were more closely aligned with theirs, but because he saw a crowd more easily manipulated with anger and emotion. Perhaps he even saw one more gullible. But before delving into how a hedonistic playboy of the variety often responsible for a few abortions themselves became a born-again pro-lifer, an examination of just what makes the stance so fundamentally Christian in the first place is required.

The Bible itself is ambiguous on the procedure, appearing at least once to recommend it as a solution to an unwanted pregnancy, while condemning the cause of any death in other areas, most notably in the sixth commandment, 'Thou shalt not kill'. The Book of Numbers chapter 5 outlines the procedure for inducing a miscarriage if a man suspects his wife has been unfaithful: he takes her to the priest who makes her drink a special concoction known as 'bitter waters' (lemon and lime included?) and if she has indeed strayed, the brew will cause her to miscarry. This is an abortion. This is prescribed by the Bible. Notably however, it is not the woman's choice but a punishment inflicted upon her by her husband and the Rabbi for perceived infidelity. That lack of choice is probably more to the point.

On the other hand, in the laws outlined in Exodus there is the death penalty for men who cause a miscarriage by accidentally striking a pregnant woman during a brawl: apparently Moses and his refugees were a rowdy lot. The perennially misspelled Deuteronomy asserts that, 'I have set before you life and death, blessings and curses. Now choose life, so that you and your children may live.' This can be taken a number of ways but at least encourages the idea of life and procreation. On the whole then, God comes out against murder; but therein lies the argument of what constitutes murder? At best one could sum up the Bible's attitude towards abortion as similar to Bill Clinton's recommendation, that they should be 'safe, legal and rare.' But apparently evangelicals don't like Clinton because he was an adulterer. Yeah, more on that later.

Evangelicals disagree. Yet while their own lily-white embryos are sacrosanct, they care little for brown ones half a world away. Trump's evangelicals love a good war: bomb a few Arabs, blow up some children's wards and it's all 'collateral damage'; they and the Republicans seek to undermine women's health clinics, public health initiatives, poverty programs and welfare at home and abroad, showing they care little for a child after it is born, yet are selectively outraged about the rights of the unborn. They love their firearms, even though suicide by gun remains a leading cause of death, gang wars plague inner-city housing projects, mass shootings occur pretty much weekly and toddlers dying in gun accidents is a common, entirely avoidable tragedy.

So is it possible to be pro-guns, pro-war and pro-life? Trump doesn't care, but he knows he can grab the attention of those who feel deeply about one without considering too carefully the others. It's called cognitive dissonance and like any good conman, Donald Trump preys on those who suffer from the condition.

Running as a Republican, Trump had to come out early and hard against abortion as it is one of their core platforms and one that excites the base. Naturally, he claimed he would support bills that limit a woman's right to choose. During the 2016 campaign when asked in a television interview he even went as far as to suggest punishment for women who get abortions. In the presidential debates later that year he invoked the bloody imagery used by so many hick pastors to fire up their flocks, boldly claiming babies were being 'ripped from their mothers' wombs' to a somewhat shocked audience and press corps.

Under Republican-held legislatures many states have steadily chipped away at women's reproductive rights, closing clinics and raising legislative and administrative hurdles that make abortion difficult to seek. Trump gloated in a tweet: 'We have come very far in the last two years with 105 wonderful new Federal Judges (many more to come), two great new Supreme Court Justices, the Mexico City Policy, and a whole new & positive attitude about the Right to Life.' The Mexico City Policy, also known as the Gag Rule, restricts American aid to foreign NGOs that counsel abortion as part of their women's health plan; even in cases of rape, incest or danger to the mother's life from birth complications.

Around spring of 2019, when states such as Alabama and Missouri were passing new rounds of restrictions rendering abortion all but impossible to seek in their states, going so far as to make it illegal for women to cross state lines to get on elsewhere, Trump ramped up the rhetoric again, pushing some of the vilest church-circle rumors about abortion yet: at a rally in Wisconsin the president claimed live in front of the cameras that at abortion clinics and hospitals babies were actually being killed after birth: 'The baby is born. The mother meets with the doctor.

They take care of the baby. They wrap the baby beautifully. And then the doctor and the mother determine whether or not they will execute the baby.'

It was a claim he had made before, though less descriptively and the crowd dutifully booed and hissed. Not at the blatant lie, but at the apparently evil abortionists allowing this atrocity to continue. Trump has amply demonstrated that he is not only willing to co-opt the values of the religious right in order to curry their favor but to peddle the worst lies and rumors that circulate in their paranoid congregations.

It emboldened the pro-life movement and legislatures. Georgia passed the 'Heartbeat Bill,' making abortion illegal after an embryo's heartbeat can be detected – around the six-week mark and before most women know they're pregnant. These cutbacks on dates (a few years ago it was 'partial-birth abortions' an emergency late-term procedure usually to save the life of the mother) are intended to whittle down the permissible time until presumably even emergency contraceptives such as the morning after pill are excluded. The very week of the 'wrapped in blankets' speech, Alabama passed some of the most draconian laws since abortion was made legal in the 1970s, outlawing the practice even in cases of rape and incest. These restrictions, as reported by Haaretz and other news agencies that conducted brief comparisons, were tighter than either Iran or Saudi Arabia.

In 2024 as Trump's second run heated up, the Supreme Court he had stacked in his first term handed the Evangelical base a massive win, effectively ending the nation's commitment to legal abortions through Roe v. Wade and allowing states to decide how to the handle the matter on their own. Immediately a raft of hardline laws making any form of abortion virtually illegal came into effect across the South and Midwest. In states from Kentucky to Alabama to Texas it became virtually impossible for women to get the procedure, even after being raped, victims of incest or if known medical complications from childbirth were likely to endanger their lives or that of their infant. In many states women are now obliged to give birth even when they know their fetus will be stillborn.

The public backlash, especially among women voters, was palpable. In states where abortion protections made it onto statewide election ballots, otherwise conservative women came out in droves to vote against measures that would erode their existing reproductive rights. This happened even as state legislatures began to set their sights on contraception measures such as the Morning After Pill. The Trump campaign responded by pressuring other Republican candidates to tone down their hard line stance and release public statements designed to placate both sides. This is likely not possible. Candidate Trump is free to talk out both sides of his mouth. President Trump will have to oversee an administration that supports either stricter or laxer laws around the subject. If the first term is any indication, he will choose the former.

The evangelical movement is a powerful minority in the US but a minority nonetheless. Outside its southern and rural strongholds, support for women, the LGBT community, desegregation and reproductive rights is stronger than ever and continues to rise. Yet thanks to identity politics, voter restrictions and gerrymandering, the evangelicals hold majorities in state legislatures disproportionate to their numbers. They are largely a single-issue block, so fired up over the abortion issue they will choose any pro-life candidate.

Still, Trump's faux piety is a ploy to keep these voters on side and he'll continue to pretend he is a man of God to do so. He even attempted an outreach to a largely African American congregation church in Detroit in June of 2024. The campaign stop backfired somewhat when it became apparent most of the local congregation were not there and his audience was largely made up of white supporters from other districts or even out of state. He followed up, most impiously a few days later with a visit as keynote speaker at the Turning Point USA convention run by well-known white supremacist Charlie Kirk.

Nobody should be fooled then, by the sight of the former and aspiring president, strapped for cash, standing in front of the cameras and half-heartedly hawking his new signed bible – his most obvious blasphemy so far. Trump has flip-flopped on individual religious issues but has largely remained committed to keeping his white Christian base on side. However he has been insincere from the start and quite cynically courted their support not out of any personal conviction but to secure their votes. Worse by claiming to be serving God, while clearly working only for himself, he is in constant and blatant violation of the Third commandment. Shifting his stance on abortion, guns, religious education and the separation of Church and State are all par for the course and through it all he has consistently invoked God's name and solicited the backing of religious figures such as mega church pastors and bible-thumping congressmen. Yet there can be no clearer or more public example of an individual profiting off God's name than the sight of Donald Trump trying to sell a personally signed Bible. At least he held it upright this time.

4.   THOU SHALT KEEP THE SABBATH HOLY

'When the term Executive Time is used, I am generally working, not relaxing. In fact, I probably work more hours than almost any past President...'

- Lethargies, 7:13

At first glance, the fourth commandment looks like it may be the only one Donald Trump has kept. He does not work on the Sabbath. He spends most weekends at golf, usually at his mar-a-Largo resort in Florida or another of his properties in Washington D.C. or New Jersey, flown back at forth at tremendous government expense. Leaving aside that this rest day should be used for something Godly: distributing alms to the poor, building a new tabernacle, kicking over money-lenders' tables or giving burning bushes the cold shoulder, one can at least say Trump is paying lip service to the Good Book. But The Donald does not just abstain from work on the Sabbath: he does precious little the rest of the week either, making him quite possibly the laziest president in the history of the Republic.

In or out of office, about half the former president's 'work' day is spent binge-watching Fox News and tweeting smack-talk about his various social media rivals, seeing his advisors and children about private business matters he was supposed to have divested himself of and if he has any sense, consulting his lawyers about the mounting barrage of legal challenges and congressional investigations coming his way. This lack of actual work makes his day off on the Sabbath superfluous. This we should take as a violation of the spirit of the Bible's Fourth Commandment, which surely insisted on a day of rest with the presumption that the remainder of the week was spent doing something productive. You know, like sacrificing first-born children, massacring Philistines or ravishing slave women. Look it up, it's all in there.

Time to take a look at how unproductive Trump's presidency really was. In early 2019, a White House staffer leaked a copy of the president's monthly schedule. Those weaned on The TV show The West Wing, with its buzzing press room, lively offices and president who worked from dawn until midnight with barely a minute to spare between scheduled engagements might have been surprised to learn that Donald Trump works far less than the average person, period. Those who knew Donald Trump were probably not surprised at all.

The leaked document revealed a staggeringly light workload for a man with the world's most powerful job. Considering the president must at least in part formulate policy for aspects of the economy, infrastructure, health services, taxation the military and foreign relations, President Trump's average workday looked like a part-timer working from home. Though he started at 5:30 most days his mornings were effectively blocked off until around 11:00 am. As he was usually finished taking appointments or attending functions by 4 pm, that's about half the day. Nevertheless he is reputedly often up till late, apparently watching TV, eating buckets of KFC and throwing tantrums on social media. By midnight he turns it in, and by anyone's standard, this schedule 24/7 for an overweight seventy-year-old must be extremely taxing. Though much of this time is spent serving himself rather than the country it, he is permanently sleep-deprived which means on any given day, likely cognitively impaired, making it a plus he doesn't do much real work.

Though he woke up at around four or five each day, he spent spending the morning's 'executive time' watching Fox News and frequently calling in to comment. Those long mornings in the West Wing were devoted to his own hobbies and interests: because Twitter feeds carry a date and time we know he spent much of the first couple of hours tweeting, usually in the maintenance of some feud or other he has with another politician, a celebrity or a news outlet. Then he spent a few hours watching morning shows such as Fox and Friends. We know this because he frequently called in live on air to clear something up, put in a good word for himself or go on a tiresome, paranoid and sometimes self-incriminating rant. He has been known to do the same for Fox host Sean Hannity's evening show. These clips are all freely available on YouTube.

President Trump apparently preferred single-page summaries that mentioned his own name a lot to keep him interested. His sons or daughter might stop by to update him on the business ventures he was supposed to be divested of to avoid conflicts of interest between his private gain and what is best for the nation. For a few hours Trump then role-played at being president, holding the odd meeting with congressmen, staffers, cabinet members or getting on the phone to foreign leaders. By 4:00 pm his poor brain would have been overtaxed. If there were no state occasions or trucker-cap hate rallies to attend, he returned to the TV and the telephone, calling into Fox again, chatting up his Russian crush Vladimir Putin in Moscow or, the leaks reliably inform us, complaining because he couldn't get porn on the White House cable channels.

If it sounds bad enough that 60% of the president's awake time was spent not working, consider that a president is expected to be available for a lot more time than the rest of us. The world's most powerful man must be available 24/7 to manage crises, and other presidents have been known to take short holidays and shorter weekends. Not so the Donald. Most weekends were and still are spent either at one of his own golf clubs outside the capital or at another Trump resort, Mar-a-Lago in Florida. The 45th president once complained about how many rounds of golf his predecessor played – around seventy a year –

but almost tripled the total himself in his first year. The fact that he and his entourage – staff, bodyguards, vehicles and canine patrols – must make this trip so frequently means a huge amount of government spending. As of January 2020, the bill stood at around $150 million. As former president, Trump still enjoys Secret Service protection that amounts to tens of millions a year. This, reports Amelia Christnot of Secondnexus, equals around 600,000 per trip, making Trump America's tenth-highest paid 'athlete'.

Given that these trips patronized his own clubs that means the US government was not only subsidizing Trump's lavish time off but injecting cash into his businesses as well. Foreign dignitaries contributed to the graft by staying at his hotels in order to curry favor. His hotels doubled their income from $33 million to $60 million in the year following his election; Trump actually doubled the membership fees for the Florida resort from $100,000 to $200,000 because he knew those who wanted to be close to the president would be willing to grease his palm.

So while Trump may be terminally lazy in the presidential role, he seems have put a good amount of effort into bilking the government out of taxpayer money. His clubs and resorts earned millions more than usual in the first two years of his presidency, not only because he increased fees or attracted more foreign dignitaries and businessmen with his office, but because he insisted on frequenting them with all the government resources allocated to the head of state.

One might forgive the president for taking a 'hard-earned' day off on the Sabbath (and on the government's dime) but it is hard to make excuses for the time wasted when he was actually at the White House and supposed to be working. The Twitter receipts show that no time of the day was too sacred to comment on some opponent or perceived rival and comparisons of the presidential schedule, along with eyewitness reports, show he was tweeting or calling into Fox when he was supposed to be in other meetings and briefings. What could be so important as to tug the leader of the free world away from the business of running it? Most of it was spent tweeting about important developments involving political opponents, basketball stars and his own intelligence:

12:49 PM - Jan 3, 2018: Korean Leader Kim Jong Un just stated that the 'Nuclear Button is on his desk at all times.' Will someone from his depleted and food starved regime please inform him that I too have a Nuclear Button, but it is a much bigger & more powerful one than his, and my Button works!

12:27 AM - Jan 7, 2018: Actually, throughout my life, my two greatest assets have been mental stability and being, like, really smart. Crooked Hillary Clinton also played these cards very hard and, as everyone knows, went down in flames. I went from VERY successful businessman, to top T.V. Star.....

12:30 AM - Jan 7, 2018: ....to President of the United States (on my first try). I think that would qualify as not smart, but genius....and a very stable genius at that!

*It apparently took three more minutes to tap a mere 26 words to finish this sentence

12:49 AM - Feb 28, 2018: WITCH HUNT!

10:19 PM - Mar 22, 2018: Crazy Joe Biden is trying to act like a tough guy. Actually, he is weak, both mentally and physically, and yet he threatens me, for the second time, with physical assault. He doesn't know me, but he would go down fast and hard, crying all the way. Don't threaten people Joe!

9:18 AM - Apr 26, 2018: MAGA!

3:31 AM - May 31, 2018: Bob Iger of ABC called Valerie Jarrett to let her know that 'ABC does not tolerate comments like those' made by Roseanne Barr. Gee, he never called President Donald J. Trump to apologize for the HORRIBLE statements made and said about me on ABC. Maybe I just didn't get the call?

11:13 AM - Jul 4, 2018: After having written many bestselling books, and somewhat priding myself on my ability to write, it should be noted that the Fake News constantly likes to pore over my tweets looking for a mistake. I capitalize certain words only for emphasis, not b/c they should be capitalized!

3:37 PM - Aug 4, 2018: Lebron James was just interviewed by the dumbest man on television, Don Lemon. He made Lebron look smart, which isn't easy to do. I like Mike!

12:23 PM - Nov 22, 2018: Brutal and Extended Cold Blast could shatter ALL RECORDS - Whatever happened to Global Warming?

11:58 PM - Dec 21, 2018: The Democrats are trying to belittle the concept of a Wall, calling it old fashioned. The fact is there is nothing else's that will work, and that has been true for thousands of years. It's like the wheel, there is nothing better. I know tech better than anyone

If Trump considers this 'working' perhaps he should give us a rest from the Twitter storms at the weekend as well. The content displays little interest in policy and a lot of concern for his ego. The range of hours alone demonstrates a man who spends far too much time worrying about what others think of him and not enough working. Or sleeping for that matter. Though in defense of his health habits, he clearly still manages to eat copiously.

If personal habits seem like a subjective measure of work ethic, the numbers are rather more telling. Apart from federal judiciary seats, which the Republican Senate was determined to stack with as many right-wing activist judges as possible, many posts remained unfilled two years into the first term. An administration is supposed to appoint ambassadors and diplomats, infrastructure overseers, military commanders and disaster-relief administrators. Hundreds of seats sat empty in civil posts, diplomatic missions and the Pentagon. As of May 2019 – two years into the administration – the unfilled cabinet posts were Homeland Security Director and Secret Service Director after the previous one was dismissed for disloyalty; Immigration and Customs Enforcement Director and *Secretary of Defense*; disaster management agency FEMA had no director (see chapter six); Secretary of the Interior, UN Ambassador and White House Chief of Staff. The people who held these offices either resigned or were fired. In cases such as the chief of staff which has seen several high-profile resignations already, no more qualified volunteers could be found and it was retained by an acting chief, Mick Mulvaney. Not only did the president show little interest in filling posts, but he had a hard time holding onto them. The staff turnover rate at the Trump White House was over three times that of any previous presidency.

Such rank incompetence in the White House was not unnoticed by its staff, many of whom were seasoned operators with work for previous administrations under their belt. They were used to dealing with driven, dedicated leaders who have a vision for the country and a schedule full of foreign dignitaries, press briefings, policy meetings, phone calls, public events and well, work. Their natural response to a spoilt, fat rich-boy sitting in the office pretending to be president was to leak like a sieve, so we have the president's people themselves to thank for knowledge of his lax schedule and TV habits. Thanks also to the leaks, and some comments by high-profile members of the administration and cabinet, we now know his attitude when he is ostensibly working is not much better: inattentive, distracted by social media, unaware, unimpressed. For a man whose entire world revolves around himself, running the rest of the world (or at least the 'free' one) is too heavy a responsibility.

The secretary of State is America's foreign minister. He or she must meet other countries' ministers, secretaries and leaders, deliver policy, be a spokesperson for the country abroad, ink treaties and memoranda, smile and shake a lot of hands and generally keep an eye on America's public image abroad. Storied names such as Henry Kissinger, Madeleine Albright, Colin Powell and Hillary Clinton have occupied the post: career diplomats, former soldiers, public servants and politicians themselves. So it seemed a bit of a step down, not to mention a policy signal when Trump appointed Exxon oilman Rex Tillerson as his first Secretary of State. It came as even more of a surprise when Tillerson turned out to be halfway competent, having at least a background in shaking hands and inking deals with presidents, prime ministers, generalissimos, kings, princes, and sheiks. Tillerson knew how the world worked and had an idea or two about working with it.

Not so his boss. As much as Tillerson tried to inform him on matters such as the security situation around North Korea, the motives of the Russians, the Venezuelan economy, Middle East conflicts and trade policy with allies and rivals, the president's swung between disinterested 'you deal with it' attitude and bold, unrealistic demands made on the spur of the moment, created frustration in Tillerson and tension. In one notable meeting with Russian leader Vladimir Putin, Tillerson claimed the president was woefully underprepared, not having bothered to read the briefings or bone up on his counterpart. At the time CNN reported, 'Over the past several days, Trump has been presented with a large binder of preparation materials for his trip to Europe, but the section on his meeting with Putin amounts to only a 'few pages' of paper, according to one White House official. A second official said each talking point is only a sentence or two long to keep Trump focused during his meeting.'

Putin reportedly ran circles around the uninformed American leader, causing consternation among his better-informed secretaries and aides. In another instance, regarding negotiations with North Korean dictator, Kim Jong-Un, Trump publicly pronounced, 'I don't think I have to prepare very much. It's about attitude, it's about willingness to get things done. So this isn't a question of preparation, it's a question of whether or not people want it to happen, and we'll know that very quickly.' His disdain for proper diplomatic channels did not stop there. Despite sending Tillerson to speak with the North Koreans,

Trump followed up with the Tweet: 'I told Rex Tillerson, our wonderful Secretary of State, that he is wasting his time trying to negotiate with Little Rocket Man.'

A few days earlier, according to one leak, the secretary of State had referred to the president as 'a fucking moron.' In a 2019 House Intelligence Committee briefing, Tillerson also informed Congress that the president's shoot-from-the-hip decisions often amounted to breaking the law. Not content to appoint son-in-law and fellow dodgy New York real-estate developer Jared Kushner to a key foreign policy role, the president demanded things of his staff that simply could not be done. He later famed it thus: 'So often, the president would say here's what I want to do and here's how I want to do it and I would have to say to him, Mr. President I understand what you want to do but you can't do it that way. It violates the law.' Within a year, the secretary had resigned, replaced by the experienced and suitably hawkish former CIA Director Mike Pompeio. In response to Tillerson's 2019 statements, the previously 'wonderful secretary of state' was now in the president's words, 'dumb as a rock.'

Other important figures have had equally damning things to say about the president's ability and work ethic since leaving his service. Former chief of staff and retired general John Kelly referred to Trump as an 'idiot' and 'unhinged'; former senior counselor and architect of his election campaign Steve Bannon assures us that rather than a brilliant businessman, Trump is 'just another scumbag'; he also reliably informs us that Trump's oldest daughter Ivanka, former shoe saleswoman and now brand ambassador for the administration is as 'dumb as a brick'. Trump's second national security adviser H. R. McMaster, also a retired military officer, referred to the president as a 'dope' with 'the intelligence of a kindergartner'; Retired General Jim Mattis, who also served as Secretary of Defense, tells us Trump has 'the understanding of a fifth or sixth-grader.' Economic adviser Gary Cohn assessed him as, 'dumb as shit.'

These could be dismissed as merely disgruntled employees, and some near the top have had their own scandals. Yet most of these figures had decades of public service under their belts and were used to dealing with leaders of a certain caliber. It is telling so many use synonyms for 'stupid' to describe the singular ignorance of the 45th president. He has shown scant willingness to learn either.

Other leaks have cataloged inattentiveness: texting and tweeting during important briefings, leaving meetings to go and watch his favorite news shows for mention of his own name, storming out of one infrastructure policy negotiation with congressional Democrats, allegedly because he was offended by their investigations of him, but just as likely because he couldn't handle the details. Briefings are handed or read to him in a single-page form, with short sentence summaries that mention his name often to keep his attention. Donald J. Trump wanted very much to *be* president, but had no interest in *doing* the job.

Yet hidden in this intellectual incurious and administratively ineffectual style of leadership could be Trump's saving grace – the less he does, the less harm he can do. As a case in point, when the Trump White House rolled out its latest Middle-East 'peace plan' under the guidance of his unqualified son-in-law, the results were predictable: the proposal simply gave the Israeli side whatever it wanted, paving the way for the right-wing Netanyahu government to step up its seizures of Palestinian land. The parties immediately started clashing again, with the first deaths reported within hours of the announcement. Pro tip: if further fighting is the response to a peace plan then it's probably not a very good one. There are other reasons not to let Trump get carried away doing any actual work.

Among other things, the president is the keeper of the nuclear codes. At almost all times, a military aide is on standby with a briefcase containing the launch codes for America's formidable arsenal of missiles and bombers, the so-called 'nuclear football.' In this holdover scenario from the cold war, the idea is that should America go to war with a nuclear-armed enemy, or be about to suffer a nuclear strike, the president can quickly authorize retaliation and the resultant global annihilation we all fear. That fear has multiplied in the hands of a man who is so sharp he refers to himself as a 'very stable genius'. Not only do observers and those close to him believe Trump lacks the judgment to handle such a responsibility, but the mounting political and legal scandals might prompt him to start a conflict of any sort in order to deflect. His assassination of a key Iranian commander in Baghdad came in the middle of impeachment hearings and echoed his own claims from several years earlier that he believed then-president Obama would 'start a war with Iran to get re-elected.' We shouldn't expect a man who advertizes his name in gold every chance he gets to be any more subtle about his intentions.

The signs of creeping madness were growing too serious to ignore as the train wreck of Trump's presidency gathered speed. His erratic behavior, incoherent speech, garbled tweets, frequent misuse of words and tendency to waffle off-topic call to mind every case of budding dementia we've seen in elderly relatives. Psychologists across the nation have suggested that the 45th president shows signs of paranoid delusion, malignant narcissism and Alzheimer's disease. Usually silent on a president's mental fitness to lead, American mental health professionals have stepped forward in their thousands to warn that the president was dangerously unstable. Psychology Today has published several articles to the effect, citing experts all the way up to storied Yale Psychiatry professor Bandy Lee. A book released in 2019, *The Dangerous Case of Donald Trump,* gave the starkest warning yet of a man who is not only unfit for office but possibly incapable of carrying out his duties. In early 2018 an anonymous whistleblower (later identified as Homeland security Chief of staff Miles Taylor) penned an open letter in the New York Times suggesting cabinet members had at least once considered removing Trump from office.

Trump's incompetence appears to be a good thing to a point: because as president he was lazy, bored by policymaking and diplomacy, and only mentioned foreign leaders when it suits him to distract from his troubles at home, his disengagement may have led to a curious state of peace. Not world peace in the sense that all the little brushfire conflicts and proxy wars ended, but in that America for a while suspended its favorite pastime of starting new scraps. 2017 saw the Trump administration bomb a couple of airfields in Syria in response to Assad's chemical attacks on his own people; in 2018, the president saw fit to tear up a treaty that had Iran agree to suspend pursuit of nuclear weapons, later rattling his limp orange saber at the Islamic Republic again by assassinating a troublesome intelligence chief in Baghdad. Trump only did the former because he felt compelled to undo any progress his predecessor had made and the latter because impeachment talk was in the news at home.

Other presidents of the past forty years have been considerably more hawkish: over two terms Reagan invaded Grenada, bombed Libya and fought a pitched naval battle with Iran. George H.W. Bush had only one term but managed to squeeze in an invasion of Panama, the First Gulf War, and a combat expedition to restore humanitarian aid in Somalia. Bill Clinton inherited Somalia, bombed the Serbians in defense of both Bosnia in his first term and later Kosovo in his second and still found time to lob a few missiles at Iraq and Sudan. The next Bush started his presidency with invasions of Afghanistan and Iraq which both outlasted his two terms. Obama wound up drawing down from Iraq but stayed in Afghanistan, before eventually getting caught up in the battle with the Islamic State terror group in Syria, forcing him to deploy troops to Iraq again. While America still has forces in Afghanistan and the Middle East, the country has not notably picked any new squabbles. Donald Trump never had any real stomach for war, not least because it means more actual work.

In many cases, leakers claimed that off-the-cuff orders that violate the constitution or just plain break state or federal laws had to be ignored. On occasions when Trump told border officers they could get rough with migrants, superiors swept the room afterward reminding the cops they most certainly could not; when aids were given orders they just could not follow they didn't. Because Trump is so easily distracted by social media or cable news, he soon forgets what he instructed subordinates to do, or fails to follow up to see if they have done it.

Nevertheless, the president's laziness and inattentiveness have raised consternation and rumors persist that in at least one point in his administration, acting FBI director Andrew McCabe discussed removing the president. The mechanism for doing this is the 25th Amendment to the Constitution, which allows the cabinet to assume power should the president be incapacitated.

This amendment was passed after the Kennedy assassination left a sudden gap in leadership and was famously used when George W. Bush signed over authority to his vice president for the short period he was anesthetized for surgery. It also allows for the cabinet to 'seize' power should the president be demonstrably unfit to lead. The amendment states that presidential responsibilities will pass to the vice president, 'In case of the removal of the president from office, or of his death, resignation, or inability to discharge the powers and duties of the said office.' This is not the same as impeachment, which is a drawn-out legal process rather like a court battle to be brought against a president for wrongdoing: this is simply marching him off in a straight-jacket, and Trump's people actually considered it.

Tellingly, for his second run, Trump has not chosen such competent public servants. Instead, he surrounded himself with yes-men and sycophants, the kind of people not to challenge his darker impulses. If elected again, he won't work and they might not either. Loyalty has trumped experience of understanding and the country may be in for a rough ride.

While President Trump did a pretty good job of 'keeping the Sabbath' and every other day free, it is fair to say that in spirit, he undermined the very need for one. Rather than working hard all week and taking a day off to reflect as God likely intended, Trump spent most of the week goofing off from the tough business of 'presidenting' and only occasionally popped his head out of the twitter stall for a meeting or a foreign trip or to attend a rally in his own honor. Yet this may be a blessing in disguise. As Churchill once said of the Americans, 'They'll do what's right after they've exhausted every other option. While Trump is lazy and distracted he cannot force his shaky, unguided hand into world affairs, causing potentially far more damage than his absence does.

5.   HONOR THY FATHER AND THY MOTHER

'My father is German, was German, born in a very wonderful place in Germany so I have a very great feeling for Germany.'

- Achomlishments 1:21

Assuming Donald Trump's parents were greedy shits like him, he may be doing a fair job of fulfilling the fifth commandment as well, but it's unlikely any parent would have wanted their son to turn out quite as amoral as The Donald. There is ample evidence that both his father and grandfather were ambitious, no-nonsense types, but also the type who would expect him to excel; to take the fortune he inherited and do more and better with it. On that count, his father must have seen what a disappointment his son was even in his own lifetime. His mother might have found other grounds for regret.

The legend of Donald Trump, storied real-estate developer and alleged self-made man, is that he started his rise to success in the early seventies with 'a small personal loan of about a million dollars,' from his father. Fred Trump was already a successful developer and slum lord, owning buildings all over Queens and the Bronx, where he was known for tenancy violations, poor conditions and disallowing African Americans from renting at his complexes. In 1973, Donald and his father were even sued by the US Justice Department for violating the Civil Rights act in their discriminatory housing practices. Yes, like his son, Fred Trump was quite possibly a racist.

One imagines the Ku Klux Klan as a strictly Southern organization but in fact, it has had chapters all over the US at one time or another. In 1927 it even held a march in New York City, white hoods and all. What is remarkable is the father of a sitting president of the United States took part in this rally – white hood and all.

The cause was supposedly populist and libertarian: to protect protestant New Yorkers from harassment by a largely Catholic police force. There may even have been some truth to it, though only about as much as Charlottesville's 'Jews will not replace us' rally ninety years hence: it was all in their minds. When the police ordered the parade to disperse, a number of the participants – let's call them 'good people on both sides' – refused to do so, leading to a number of arrests of what the papers called 'berobed marchers'. Fred Trump, in his early twenties at the time, was among those collared – perhaps the family's first 'white collar' crime. It is likely because he was released without charges he went on to commit many more violations throughout his career in business and real estate.

In this respect, the apple certainly hasn't fallen far from the tree. Trump has staked his political career on bigotry, from his 2012 embrace of 'birtherism,' the notion that the previous president, Barack Obama couldn't possibly be an American citizen because his father had been Kenyan, to his 2015 campaign announcement where he derided Mexicans as 'rapists,' to his refrain that refugees arrived from 'shithole countries.' Determined to go beyond merely following in his father's footsteps, racism was not the only trait young Donald mimicked: he believed he could go one over Dad in the real estate line, aiming for downtown Manhattan, the big leagues, and a place where he probably thought black people couldn't afford to live anyway.

It is no secret that the wealthy can get their kids into good schools through donations and grants. They end up paying more, but the brand value is priceless. Trump was reputed to have been a bit of a tearaway in his teens, frustrating teachers and bullying other kids, earning him a transfer to a military prep school as an adolescent, as a means of discipline. This was perhaps the first way in which he genuinely failed his parents. In university, he secured a spot at the prestigious Wharton Business School, where his professor gushingly referred to him as 'the dumbest goddamn student I ever had'. Strike two. Donald Trump may or may not have 'graduated' on his name rather than merit, but he had clearly failed to live up to his teacher's expectations. It must have been a disappointment to the family.

This should be especially galling from a man who demanded President Obama's college transcripts (after relentlessly pursuing his birth certificate), because he couldn't imagine the first black president having graduated from both Columbia and Harvard, or serving as chairman of the Harvard Law Review on his own merit. Being wealthy and connected, genuine achievement was something young Trump was apparently unfamiliar with. Despite demanding Obama's school results, Trump's own transcripts remain a state secret, as do other aspects of his academic record. Being thick as a plank is no surprise. He claims to be a genius but has demonstrably proven to be the opposite, as all those former cabinet members can attest. Likely having just coasted through on the family name, Trump, therefore, squandered an expensive education paid for by his parents by not learning a thing in school, as nobody wants a dropkick for a son, especially not the wealthy and influential.

Nevertheless he took his Wharton diploma and entered real estate, just like his father, with his 'small' loan. In today's money of course that 'small loan of a million dollars' he secured from Daddy Trump amounts to around $60 million in today's money. Inflation alone hasn't raised it that much; a change in property prices, spending power and other adjustments push the figure up. Moreover, it wasn't really just a million to begin with. Through various tricks – unpaid loans, gifted money, forgiven debts, and good old fashioned inheritance-tax dodging, Fred Trump managed to leave pretty much all his wealth to his children before he died, paying a tenth of the tax they should have upon inheritance. Donald's share alone amounted to something in the region of $400 million in today's dollars.

Not only did he manage to squeeze money out of his father, but he also managed to fool banks into lending him money. By calling into Forbes as an unnamed advisor and pretending to know Trump's real worth, he got himself on the rich list. He used that reputation to secure bank loans he may otherwise not have gotten. He also overvalued properties he owned when seeking loans, undervalued them when it came time to pay taxes and overvalued them again for insurance purposes. This is normally called fraud when people who aren't rich do it. It is also the sort of skullduggery his father Fred would probably have approved of, greasy old miser than he was. Because of all this, Trump's fortune in property may be the only thing keeping him afloat. In fact, if he had simply invested it all in property and sat on it he would still just be worth the Forbes estimate of around $4 billion he enjoys now (not the $10 billion he claims to have amassed).

So how did Trump manage not to make any more hay than he would have by doing nothing at all? Quite simply by being a shitty businessman. While he followed the advice of his crooked lawyers and accountants to squeeze more money out of banks and give less to the IRS, as mentioned earlier, any attempt at real business was a disaster. He failed at launching an airline, several luxury brands, and even at running casinos, which common sense tells us always makes money. The casinos were handy at least when Donald inevitably dishonored his rich daddy by squandering his inheritance – Fred's lawyers were known to buy millions of dollars in chips and never use them as a means of covering Donald's debts at the time and avoiding explaining how the money changed hands. Fred Died at age 93, no doubt glad he no longer had to keep bailing out his deadbeat son.

So on the first count, mixed results: Donald is certainly a chip off the old block regarding his unscrupulousness and bigotry but on the other hand an educational disappointment and financial burden in that his failures necessitated family rescue packages. In this respect, he has surely not honored his father.

And what of his dear mother? Mary Anne McLeod was born to a crofter on a small Scottish Island. Her family moved to New York and the young Mary met and married Fred Trump. Ironically she was likely an economic migrant, escaping the poverty caused by the depression and generally sparse conditions of her homeland. Trump has spent his presidency trying to slam the door shut on similar such migrants (albeit from Latin America and the Muslim world) so this is surely the most fundamental way in which he dishonors his dear mother's memory.

Trump campaigned on building a wall between the US and Mexico, and promised a complete ban on Muslims entering the country. Though being president is harder and obtaining congressional budget for the wall and federal court approval for the bans have both proven more difficult than promising it, he has still made a decent attempt to dash the hopes of hungry refugees. Asylum seekers from Latin America have been rounded up in detention camps and separated from their children; Muslims have been turned back at ports of entry or denied visas, many also being separated from loved ones stateside. Visa overstayers have been deported including US military veterans and their families.

Moreover his administration has gone after chain migration, stopping families from sponsoring the visas of their relatives and a process his own immigrant third wife Melania's parents had benefitted from; next on his list was birthright citizenship, seeking to end the opportunity for migrant children to become US citizens, as his father was allowed to be. Much of this xenophobia is encouraged by his creepy advisor Stephen Miller, who doesn't get laid much but apparently has the president's ear. This is a far cry from the plaque on the Statue of Liberty that welcomed his mother and grandfather with the offer, 'Give me your tired, your poor, your huddled masses yearning to breathe free.' The system of immigration that gave Trump life itself is a chance he gladly denies others.

Mary Trump was also pious, far more so than her fourth child Donald has turned out to be. An active churchgoer, she collected for cerebral palsy, the blind, and the intellectually disabled; volunteered at hospitals and schools and all this while the wife of a successful businessman who could have just sat around the garden drinking martinis instead. Strike two against Donald, whose 'charities' have been mere fronts for dodgy business ventures, slush funds for legal damages brought against him in said ventures and vanity projects where he could be claiming to do God's work but instead squandered money on giant portraits of his own fat orange ass. Mary passed at age 88, just a year after her husband, lucky not to have lived to see her son drag the whole country down into the sewer.

But perhaps it is neither of these that inspires Donald Trump and gives him an example to live up to. Unlike either of his parents – the bigoted, successful Fred Trump or the pious matronly Mary – Trump's paternal grandfather was actually pretty fucking cool. This is something Trump, despite trying multiple rebrandings, making cameo appearances in films and appearing in a self-deprecating Comedy Central Roast, has never been.

Friedrich Drumpf was born in 1869 in the Kingdom of Bavaria, which already sounds much more awesome than Queens: in those days, Germany was a number of separate statelets and countries. Emigrating when he was young to avoid compulsory military service (another family trait it would seem), Friedrich ended up in the United States at age sixteen, working as a barber. That's right, he worked. He operated restaurants and brothels in Seattle and its environs during the gold rush (see Commandment Six). Grandfather Trump was reported to have 'mined the miners' making his money in Washington off the gold prospectors and their needs: a room, a bed, liquor, gambling and whoring. An early precursor perhaps to Trump's penchant for selling snake oil, though booze and women were at the time a surer bet than ethereal pride in flag and forefather. He then had a role in the Yukon gold rush after Washington had tried up and made some good coin, an opportunist like his descendants. Unlike them he was a genuine self-made man.

After marrying, Drumpf tried to return to Germany. However his absence from the military rolls had been noted and he was stripped of his citizenship (Ironically again, as Trump has deported migrants who have actually served in the US military). Stateless, a refugee and an outcast, he was at least no longer named Drumpf because the American authorities apparently had trouble with spelling (potential future supporters of his grandson perhaps), Trump had nowhere else to go but back to America. At this point it should be apparent that both Donald Trump's mother and his paternal grandfather had been poor immigrants who had sought a new life in America. Both in their way had made something of themselves. This is contrasted with the casual disregard with which he uses Hispanic migrants and Muslim families as a prop for anti-immigrant fervor. In this, Donald Trump is most certainly not honoring his ancestors.

Trump's grandfather eventually laundered the fortune he'd made in gambling and whores by way of New York real estate, becoming a respectable citizen, dying at age 49 in 1918 at the onset of the influenza epidemic with a small fortune and a miserable cough. His son Fred managed to turn it into a large fortune and leave a chunk to Donald. Yet one must ask why he had to go through so much hardship, emigrating young, living rough in gold country – no doubt helping himself to those whores who worked for him – just to see his idiot grandson squander it on 'Trump Steaks' and failed casinos. In light of his own grandfather's death due to the Flu Pandemic, Trump's failed response to Covid-19 (see Chapter Six) seems especially ironic.

Perhaps in the most glaring example of Trump's failure to honor his parents, there are moments when he cannot even recall who was born where. In July 2018 when addressing the EU, and again in 2019 speaking to NATO Secretary-General Jens Stoltenberg, Trump proudly announced his father Fred had been born in Germany. While this is true of his grandfather, it seems a silly mistake to make about his father who was born and lived his whole life in Queens; it is especially silly to have done so twice. Surely part of honoring one's ancestors entails remembering where the hell they came from. Some shrinks pointed to this and around the same time, his inability in one speech to say 'origins' (pronounced several times as 'oranges' before he gave up altogether) as signs of creeping dementia. A handy excuse for when he finally meets St. Peter perhaps.

The road to the Pearly Gates may lead through Donald's treatment of other family members. When his first wife Ivana passed away at the age of 73, he and their eldest children, Eric, Ivanka and Don Jr, had her buried at Trump's Bedminster golf course, possibly in or around the 19th hole. It might seem strange to have buried the woman he divorced three decades prior on his property, but they did share three adult children and several grandchildren. It was widely speculated at the time that because under New Jersey law, properties used as cemeteries can be exempt from property taxes, this was just a cheap trick to fiddle the books. It is not known whether Trump lodged any sort of application on this front. Either way, Ivana Trump was buried in a corner of the back yard, like a pet that had been struck by a car, with little but a plain plaque to remember her by. A few months later, pictures circulated on the internet of the gravesite neglected and overgrown. The Bible does not specifically call for deference to former spouses, but surely that would be in the spirit of the family-centric Fifth Commandment.

While they share some traits, it is fair to say that Trump is not entirely cut from the same cloth as his forebears. Whether the cause is property, pioneering, prostitution or philanthropy, Donald Trump has proved a failure, an underachiever or a common trickster. His grandfather was a trailblazer, his father a self-made billionaire, his mother a pious giver, while Donald is merely an inheritor, pretending he did it all himself and falling short whenever he was at the helm. In this sense, Donald Trump has not lived up to the promise, expectations or potential of his ancestors. His father would likely have wanted to see him succeed in business and education, but Trump is probably no wealthier in real terms than what he inherited and certainly no smarter; while his mother was a pious and charitable woman,

Trump's own sleazy 'foundation' made a mockery of the very concept of giving. His grandfather was a penniless migrant who helped build the country, but Trump seeks to stop others from having the same opportunity. He has not honored them as the Bible commands.

6.   THOU SHALT NOT KILL

'I could stand in the middle of Fifth Avenue and shoot somebody and I wouldn't lose voters.'

-    Armalites, 1:1

It is safe to say Donald Trump has never personally killed anyone. It's hard for the most powerful leader not to drop a few bombs here and there, or bump off a terrorist, or approve a hit on some inconvenient strongman. Given that the power to wage war is so frequently used by the holders of that office it is almost impossible to say an American president does not have blood on his hands.

The most peaceful of recent presidents Jimmy Carter is still widely derided by chickenhawks on the right for being a sissy because he never started an actual war. Yet when Iranian revolutionaries seized over fifty hostages at the American embassy in 1979, this so-called wimp sent Special Forces troops on a rescue mission. Unfortunately, an aircraft accident in the Iranian desert killed several servicemen and the military aborted the mission. So at least Carter was up for a fight, despite having poor luck at it.

Trump has been closer to Carter in this respect. While most of his predecessors have championed wars cold and hot (see chapter four), Trump lobbed a few ineffectual missiles at Syria over a humanitarian grudge and maintained a US military presence since the Obama administration to fight Iraq's ISIS and Afghanistan's Taliban among others. In October 2019, a Special Forces raid killed the head of ISIS in Syria even while America was drawing down its presence. In Afghanistan his administration also negotiated a drawdown deal with the Taliban ultimately seen out by his successor.

So compared to the carnage of the past few decades Trump's tenure has been relatively light overseas, and has largely been a continuation of wars inherited from previous administrations. The danger in his domestic posture comes in many forms: from the innate racism and bigotry that encourages violence in others, to the inhumane treatment of migrants on the southern border to his terrible record on public health, especially that of women. Worse still, his deliberate and willful mishandling of the deadliest pandemic in a hundred years vastly increased the death toll among ordinary Americans.

As a young man, Trump avoided the compulsory military service that could have seen him shipped to Vietnam. Securing several deferments, including one medical for alleged 'bone spurs' in his heel (he can never recall which one) he spent the late sixties at college, partying and waiting out the clock. So unlike some of his political opponents in later life, including presidential hopeful John McCain, who spent five years as a POW after his fighter plane was shot down over Vietnam, or Special Prosecutor Robert Mueller who had been a decorated infantry officer wounded in combat, Trump never had the opportunity to potentially kill someone in person. It didn't stop him calling on his home state to kill others.

One morning in 1989, New York police found a severely injured woman who had been beaten, raped and left for dead in Central Park. Gangs of youths had been known to rob passersby and had been active during the night, and five suspects were hauled in for this particular crime, all black and Latino teenagers. The victim awoke from a coma a couple of weeks later with no recollection. It took eighteen months and two trials to convict the 'Central Park Five,' apparently with a lot of coerced confessions and confused details.

During the trial, local big shot real estate developer Donald Trump (at the time during his eight-year financial losing streak, which might have made him more bitter) took out a full-page advertisement in the papers demanding a return of the death penalty, which the state of New York no longer issued at the time. The one time Trump was willing to spend $85,000 promoting something other than himself, was when he called for the execution of teenagers who had been framed. 'They should be forced to suffer.' He wrote, and then told TV interviewer Larry King, 'Maybe hate is what we need if we're going to get something done.'

Over a decade later the five convicted offenders were acquitted when the real rapist was identified – a serial predator already serving time for other crimes. Trump didn't mind being wrong: in a 2002 opinion piece he wrote, 'Settling doesn't mean innocence. Speak to the detectives on the case and try listening to the facts. These young men do not exactly have the pasts of angels.'

It was a primer for Trump's future campaigns. He staked his first presidential run in 2012 on the 'birther' conspiracy theory, which held that then-president Barack Obama could not be a citizen because his father was Kenyan (which was true) and that he had been born overseas (patently false). When Trump announced his 2016 run from the gilded escalator of his Manhattan tower, he derided undocumented migrants as 'rapists' and drug dealers and complained Mexico was 'not sending their best people.'

Trump found an outlet for that prejudice in a solid white base of 'conservatives' and 'evangelicals'. His pre- and post-election rallies attracted mostly white, largely middle-aged, often Christian followers adorned in a variety of white supremacist symbols new and old: Nazi swastikas, Aryan Brotherhood tattoos and Confederate flags. Stepping into the auditorium at a Trump rally during the campaign of 2016, the air of aggression was palpable. One had to be careful what they wore: some pro-Trump paraphernalia like the infamous red hat was a safe bet. Back it up with a little flag – a Dixie one if you wanted to be especially bold – and a T-shirt with some derisory comment about Hillary Clinton or Barack Obama: 'I'd rather be a Russian than a Democrat was a popular one.' People had an eye about them like they were looking for someone who didn't fit it, someone they could heckle, jostle or outright sucker-punch. Members of the press, women in beads, someone with an anti-Trump placard, any group who looked too young, to liberal, too *urban* were potential targets.

When Trump got up on the stage, the usual suspects were targets of his rhetoric. Migrants from Latin America, the Muslim parents of an army officer killed in combat, anyone with a scarf or a turban or frankly, tits. When placard-waving dissenters chanted, Trump would exhort his fans to 'knock the hell out of them,' and promise to pay the legal bills. The candidate would holler into the microphone people who opposed him should be 'carried out on stretchers'. Reporters were assaulted, dissenters roughed up and as an African American heckler was ejected from one rally on national TV, he was sucker-punched by a white attendee.

Trump's violent campaign turned into a violent administration, the usual targets bearing the brunt. Muslims from half a dozen nations were denied entry into American ports until federal judges ruled a religiously-motivated ban unconstitutional. Overstayers and the like were rounded up and deported, even military personnel and decorated veterans of America's wars or their spouses. Other migrants and asylum seekers were rounded up at the border and herded into concentration cages. Families were separated in a deliberate effort to punish Latin American migrants: children were torn from their parents' arms and sent to separate facilities in other states. Some died in custody.

The ethnic cleansing of America began with Trump's first term and he promised to do the same in his 2024 re-election campaign. In September 2024, he loudly proclaimed on the debate stage across from his opponent Kamala Harris, that Haitian immigrants in Springfield Ohio were 'eating the cats, eating the dogs, eating the pets of the people that live there.' Though there were no such credible reports from local law enforcement, attacks on migrants in Springfield and bomb threats against facilities that housed or assisted them such as schools and hospitals spiked over the following weeks. Not content to merely spread internet disinformation about migrants, Trump also directly stated during his campaign, 'On day one, we will begin the largest domestic deportation operation in American history.'

In the summer of 2020, the nation was rocked by street protests against police brutality. In Minneapolis, a white officer had suffocated an African American suspect named George Floyd to death and the incident, captured on video, inflamed activists and advocates left and right. In cities across the country, loose affiliations of protestors such as Black Lives Matter and

Antifa challenged the authorities in street rallies that sometimes turned violent, attracting looters and other opportunists. As clashes with police escalated, cars were burned and stores were robbed, the right wing militia groups sprung into vigilante action.

In one riot in Kenosha Wisconsin, a seventeen-year-old youth name Kyle Rittenhouse brought an AR-15 assault rifle and ended up shooting a pair of protestors. He was charged and acquitted and this gentle act of white supremacy got him feted by the Republican party and earned him an audience with a sympathetic President Trump. This endorsement of white vigilantism was on brand for the champion of Birtherism.

Later in the season, when the demonstrations reached Washington DC and neared the Capitol, Trump hid in his bunker, emerging only to wave an upside-down bible about in front of a church and call on the Chairman of The Joint Chiefs, General Mark Milley, who appeared next to the President in camouflage combat fatigues, to teargas the protestors. The gas thankfully was spared, and Milley for his part, later publicly regretted the photo-op. But the attraction to violence and the tools of war that runs through the American right was placed front and center in this season of unrest.

Aside from the worship of confederate statues discussed in chapter two, there is one other inanimate object that Trump and his supporters revere, a sleek black weapon with pistol grip and curved magazine that can spit death at up to 900 rounds a minute: the good old American, assault rifle. Though Trump has never owned one, he has become the new champion of the gun lobby, America's gun culture and with it, the nation's appalling domestic death toll.

The National Rifle Association (NRA) was born in the early twentieth century to teach marksmanship and survival skills and quickly evolved into a harmless national gun club. Yet by the latter twentieth century, it had discovered a new role as powerful political lobby and defender the right to bear arms. Republican candidates up and down the country seek the organization's endorsements, many even showing off their shooting skills in TV ads or posing with firearms in their campaign posters and commercials to curry favor with the organization and its members. Love for the gun is especially strong among white rural and southern voters; the very same demographic that usually supports conservative causes and has fallen behind the cult of Trump.

As candidate Trump joked, 'I could stand in the middle of Fifth Avenue and shoot somebody and wouldn't lose any voters.' This remark elicited a hearty cheer from the auditorium at the Iowa rally where he delivered it, suggesting he was correct. Given that any random shooting in downtown Manhattan would be unlikely to strike a white rural Republican voter, it should perhaps come as no surprise this was an exciting proposition for his audience at the time.

Even more exciting was the prospect of using their beloved weapons in that most patriotic of duties, to challenge tyrants the way Paul Revere did when he rode to warn people King George was coming for their guns; or something to that effect, ask Sarah Palin. In this case however the 'tyrant' was a sixty-nine-year-old grandmother who had the audacity to challenge Trump in a general election.

One warm summer's evening during the campaign of 2016, Donald Trump warned his rally audience at Wilmington, North Carolina, that the Democrats would tighten gun laws again and that his opponent Hillary Clinton would be particularly fervent in doing so. The complaint was that as president she would pick federal judges less predisposed toward gun rights who were more likely to rubber-stamp stricter regulations, which was probably true, but not nearly serious enough to warrant his proposed remedy: 'If she gets to pick her judges, nothing you can do, folks,' Trump warned, eliciting the customary boo from his compliant fans. This was followed by the unveiled threat, 'Although the Second Amendment people...maybe there is, I don't know.'

Threatening violence was nothing new to Trump rallies, but here he was openly hinting he might be solve the problem of politicians they disagree with simply by assassinating them. He did not stop there. With poll numbers sagging in early 2019, then president Trump suggested more political violence against his opponents if they impeached him over any scandals, opposed his policies, or defeated him in the 2020 election. For all of these political outcomes, Trump's solution was simple: 'I actually think that the people on the right are tougher,' he told a Breitbart reporter, 'I can tell you I have the support of the police, the support of the military, the support of the Bikers for Trump – I have the tough people, but they don't play it tough — until they go to a certain point, and then it would be very bad, very bad.'

Trump's 'Second Amendment People' have heard the call. Hate crimes are on the rise again, with ethnic minorities such as African Americans, Jews, Muslims, Sikhs and Hispanics all frequent targets; mass shootings – classed as workplace, mall or school shootings in which more than four people are killed or wounded – have steadily increased. As Trump's impeachment on corruption charges heated up in late 2019, the calls from the right for a 'Second Civil war' became even shriller. Trump himself joined in, retweeting a Baptist pastor's warning to that effect and referring to the impeachment process as an attempted 'coup.' Militia activity spiked, with one group, the so-called Oath Keepers sharing the tweet among 24,000 followers and following it up by warning of a 'hot' civil war (spoiler: they have all the guns). During a 2020 presidential debate, while he warned his followers the vote would be rigged against them, the moderator asked if he condemned neo-fascists such as the Proud

Boys. Trump advised them to 'stand back and stand by' – prophetic in the wake of their conduct after he lost.

Hate crimes against Mosques, Synagogues and even women's health clinics reached an all-time high under Trump. The FBI reported an increase in the number of white supremacist groups and placed white supremacy as a security threat on an equal footing to that of the Islamic State. Now, more than 70% of crimes classed as domestic terrorism are not committed by the much-vilified Muslims, but by radical white men in camouflage cosplay with AR-15 rifles, nappy beards, bulging beer guts and an ethno-nationalist agenda.

Cesar Sayoc, arrested in 2018 for sending pipe bombs and making threats against Democrat senators and news stations, was an avid Trump supporter. Three men in Kansas were caught plotting to bomb a Somali American community in 2016; three more right-wing militiamen who professed support for Trump bombed a mosque in Missouri, and Nicolas Cruz, who shot up his own school and killed 17 classmates in 2018 was another Trump fan self-radicalized on the internet. To make matters worse Trump's toxic mix of people-hate and gun-love has gone international: A young man in Quebec opened fire at an Islamic Centre killing six and wounding over a dozen; in Christchurch, New Zealand a gunman killed over fifty worshippers at two mosques and was intercepted on his way to a third. Many of the victims were refugees who had escaped conflicts in South Asia and the Middle East. Both killers had professed a degree of support for Trump and his anti-immigrant, anti-Muslim rhetoric policies. Both had also been radicalized online and succumbed to America's right-wing gun culture.

Though not politically motivated, the deadliest mass shooting to date in the US occurred during Trump's first year in office. A lone gunman named Stephen Paddock fired over a thousand rounds from a hotel window into a crowd at a Las Vegas music festival, killing sixty people and wounding over 400 before turning his weapon on himself. Many of the guns found in his possession were fitted with bump-stocks, an external part that simulates full-automatic fire without turning the weapon mechanically into a machine gun, which would be illegal. This enabled Paddock to fire rapidly into the crowd, at a similar rate of fire to a military assault rifle, inflicting mass casualties. While the Trump administration initially sought to ban the sale of bump stocks after the spree, seven years later the Supreme Court bowed to right wing pressure and overturned the law, making the deadly kits available once again. Trump, ever the opportunist and seeking reelection at the time, promptly did an about face and endorsed the court's decision. Though generations of leaders have allowed America's gun problems to fester, firearms became the leading cause of death among American children during Trump's tenure. It is gratifying to know that Donald Trump plans to give the next generation of crazed gunmen the proper tools to do the job.

Trump has also palled around with known killers and human rights abusers because this behavior appeals to his red-hat followers, who fancy themselves tough guys. Similar to his kinship with Rittenhouse, He pardoned Arizona Sherriff Joe Arpaio, known for the abuse of prisoners in custody, his jail having health and sanitary conditions so poor it had been described as a concentration camp. Milwaukee Sheriff David Clarke also appeared at Trump's side several times as a poster boy for tough law enforcement. Under Clarke's oversight, his jail neglected its charges, leading to the death of at least one prisoner from dehydration after the water was shut off for days on end; He also had pregnant female suspects shackled and denied medical attention, leading to the death of a newborn infant. Chief Petty Officer Gallagher was Navy Seal whom a military court had found guilty of unlawfully killing captured guerrilla suspects in Iraq. The president pardoned Gallagher in late 2019 and to rub salt in the Pentagon's wound, he stripped Navy prosecutors of the medals they had earned for their conduct in the trial.

Not content just to please the macho 'law and order' crowd at home, Trump's admiration for tough-guy tactics has also been deployed as a tool of foreign policy or a convenient distraction. Though Trump managed a record three years without starting any new conflicts (George H.W. Bush managed to cram three invasions into his single term) the urge of the US to go to war can hardly be stifled for long, especially when a distraction is needed.

Shortly after New Year in 2020 and in the midst of his first impeachment, president Trump ordered the assassination by missile strike of the top Iranian official in Iraq, who was accused of plotting against US interests. If inflaming tensions was the desired result it worked: Iran responded two days later with missile strikes on a US airbase in the region. Tellingly, Mr. Trump himself claimed in 2011 that then president Obama would start a war with Iran to get re-elected if he were impeached. Subtlety was never this killer's strong point.

A genuine, if more insidious foreign threat reached America's shores in late 2019. On 12 March 2020, the President delivered his second televised Oval Office address three years. These are typically rare speeches in which a solemn-looking Commander-in-Chief stares down the camera from the Resolute Desk to announce grave national threats or imminent military action. In this case it was the rapid spread of the deadly COVID-19 pandemic. Viewers might have expected to see a strong, empathetic leader lay out a deliberate course of action. Instead, President Trump stuttered his way through the teleprompter, occasionally skipping half a sentence, hands continuously fidgeting on the desk.

The President exaggerated measures taken in the United States that were not yet as strict several dozen countries who had already imposed curfews, closed their borders and mobilized their national health services. While Mr. Trump claimed the epidemic response was moving 'very rapidly,' Dr Anthony Fauci, Director of the National Institute of Allergy And Infectious Diseases, testified to Congress that nobody as yet had been charged with overseeing a national testing program, and the number of infected was largely unknown.

Throughout the entire nine minutes of his address, Mr. Trump's face showed little emotion: not empathy, concern or crucially, confidence in his own command. The President came across as a man who had just picked up the paper that morning and discovered there was a viral outbreak in another country altogether. The stock market, one of Trump's preferred measures of his success as President, immediately tumbled over a thousand points. By the following Monday it had recorded its biggest losses since the crash of 1987. The Dow drop was ironic because it was in order to avoid such economic panic in the first place that the president and his cohorts had denied the seriousness of the pandemic and avoided taking drastic action. America was already six weeks late, and this had been no accident.

Well before disaster struck, the administration had already set to work undermining nationwide health programs and other government safeguards against the spread of illness. Science had never sat well with Trump, who followed gut instinct instead.

Candidate Trump jumped on the anti-green energy bandwagon: he dismissed global warming as a 'hoax' perpetuated by China to gain a competitive advantage, asserted that wind turbines were decimating the native bird population and pushed the rumor that low-frequency sound waves generated by the turbines caused cancer. Long before running for President, Trump had expressed a concern that vaccines for measles or the flu may be responsible for autism, which was a popular belief on social media sites and in church circles, but supported by scant scientific evidence. As President, he claimed with his signature bravado, 'Nobody knows more about vaccines than I do.'

Upon taking office, Trump stacked his staff and cabinet with creationists, climate-science deniers and internet alarmists. Education Secretary Betsy DeVos had challenged the teaching of evolution in schools. One of the people invited to apply for head of the regulatory Food and Drug Administration was an anti-regulation activist; another name floated for a commission on immunization safety was prominent anti-vaxxer Robert F. Kennedy Jr.

Lack of a national healthcare system makes it harder to conduct a unified pandemic response. The US has Medicare, Medicaid, the Affordable healthcare act but these often rely on coordination with private insurers, and many poor and unemployed have no cover at all. Between 2010, when the Affordable Care Act was implemented and 2017, Trump's first year in office, the Republican-led House of Representatives had voted – and failed – over seventy times to overturn 'Obamacare', to defund it or otherwise erode its provisions. In March 2020, with a new virus spreading in the continental United States, the Trump administration was still lobbying the Supreme Court to remove pre-existing conditions from the mandate, even though Trump had publicly proclaimed on dozens of occasions that he would not.

The Centers for Disease Control and Prevention (CDC) is a government laboratory monitoring infectious public health threats, working with industry to develop vaccines and treatments and advising the public. In 2017, when Congress was trying to repeal the ACA, Trump ally Mitch McConnell sponsored an failed amendment to the bill that would slash funding for the Prevention and Public Health Fund which supports the center. In 2009, The US Agency for International Development launched a pandemic early warning program. Cooperating with scientists and governments around the world, it identified over 1200 potential pandemic threats including influenza, Ebola and 160 strains of coronavirus. It trained researchers in more than 60 foreign laboratories, including the Wuhan Institute of Virology, which first identified Covid-19. Yet a few months before that event, the Trump administration had ended funding for the program, effectively closing America's contribution to a global pandemic response.

As the Coronavirus spread in March 2020, the President claimed variously that he had been unaware of some of these measures, that nobody had anticipated a pandemic, or that the cuts had come under the previous administration. Former Attorney General Susan Rice emphatically stated to CNN, 'Not only did we know it could come, we should have prepared for it to come as we did in the Obama administration, and we gave them the wherewithal to do so in the Trump administration.'

Within Trump's administration, important health and safety roles had been vacated. The Secretary of Health and Human Services resigned after misusing government resources; the deputy Communications Director of HHS resigned after making anti-Muslim comments. The CDC director quit after it came to light she held stock in tobacco companies. The Secretary of Housing and Urban Development left within the administration's first two months, as did the first Secretary of Agriculture. The administration was already on its third *Acting* Secretary of Homeland Security, and the post had not been properly staffed since 2017.

On February 24, after the WHO had reported 80,000 cases in three dozen countries, the New York Stock exchange plummeted a thousand points, its greatest fall since the Global Financial Crisis. Trump, who had in many instances touted the climbing stock market under his tenure as President, tried to calm jittery investors with over a billion dollars in emergency aid from Congress. The President's public tone betrayed his priorities as he tweeted, 'The Coronavirus is very much under control in the USA…Stock Market starting to look very good to me!'

On February 26, the President declared a new task force to deal with Coronavirus headed by Vice President Mike Pence. Pence's public health record as Indiana Governor garnered poor ratings from experts. The governor had resisted CDC appeals for a clean needle exchange program for heroin addicts, leading to a 2015 HIV outbreak that was the worst in his state's history. Pence was a notoriously religious man, adhering to a strict creationist interpretation of the Bible over science-based solutions. He began the first meeting of his task force with a group prayer.

The day after Pence was appointed, Mr. Trump falsely announced at a press conference that there had been a *reduction* in cases. 'We're going very substantially down, not up. We have it so well under control, I mean, we really have done a very good job,' the President said. The following day, Trump assured a gathering of African American leaders, 'It's going to disappear. One day, it's like a miracle, it will disappear. It could get worse before it gets better. It could maybe go away. We'll see what happens. Nobody really knows.' Cases kept flooding in and the first US death occurred on February 29.

By March 6, two dozen states had confirmed cases and several had already declared an emergency. The President flew to tornado-ravaged Tennessee where he was seen on camera shaking hands with officials and well-wishers, packing over a hundred souls into a small local church to hold an impromptu presser. A reporter asked about the social distancing requirements other states were already recommending, but Mr Trump shrugged, 'It doesn't bother me.' The handshakes and backslapping continued on his next leg, a visit to the CDC in Atlanta where Trump told the cameras the doctors were amazed 'how much I know about this stuff.' He ended the evening at his Florida resort, where he was to spend the next three days hosting fundraisers and golfing. A week later, the resort and surrounding neighborhood had accounted for over half the state's 131 confirmed cases. The white house finally implemented basic temperature checks for anyone coming near the President, but his macho denial of the danger was already filtering out to the faithful.

By March 11, the day the WHO declared Covid-19 a global pandemic, the world had recorded 126,000 cases and over 4,600 deaths. In America there were over 1,500 nationwide and there had been several dozen deaths. The President was still publicly in a state of denial. He sought to reassure senate Republicans at a Monday luncheon, telling them on camera, 'Just stay calm. It will go away.' The following day, Dr Fauci told Congress, 'Bottom line, it's going to get worse.'

On March 13, the President arrived half an hour late to his Rose Garden press conference and started shoveling blame: 'We had some very old and obsolete rules we had to live with,' he said, suggesting an insufficient holdover response plan from the previous administration. However, it was Trump's own subsequent cutbacks that had removed many of the systems and guidelines that had been put in place to deal with a pandemic response. Asked whether he took responsibility for closing the pandemic desk, the President shot back testily, 'No I don't take responsibility at all.' It wasn't long before a 2019 video surfaced in which the President candidly discussed the dismantling of the response unit.

According to a poll conducted by the Pew Center, 53% of Republican voters thought the press had 'greatly exaggerated' the virus. Only 17% thought that the media had the story right. While the WHO, CDC and medical professionals in Trump's own white house were warning people to take greater protective measures, practice social distancing and employ more rigorous hygiene, Fox News hosts dismissed the scare as a 'political weapon' or 'another attempt to impeach the President.'

Republican-led states were slowest to take action. Schools remained open and church groups still gathered; the president led by example, standing shoulder to shoulder with cabinet members and shaking hands with officials at a time when European leaders and even politicians in Canada had taken to masks, gloves and strict social distancing. By late March the US had 212,000 positive cases – the world's highest to date – with 5,000 deaths and climbing. Despite the stimulus package announced by the President in mid-March, the administration's budget continued to demand more reductions to the CDC, smaller contributions to the WHO and further cuts to welfare and food assistance.

Without an overriding health authority to coordinate national plans, each state had to source testing equipment, identify at-risk patients, provide facilities and fund it all. FEMA documents showed critical shortages of medical supplies. Washington DC had received less than 100 of the five million N95 masks requested, 1% of 200 million pairs of latex gloves and not a single body bag despite asking for 15,000. The entire country had only about 9,500 ventilators for patients in its National Strategic Stockpile, despite hospitals across the country requiring hundreds of thousands. Improvements to this were hampered by Mr Trump's brewing feud with state governors.

Maryland Governor Larry Hogan prepared emergency funding in February. Ohio Governor Mike DeWine showed initiative even before his state had reported any cases, addressing social distancing, cancelling events and preparing the medical services for increased demand. Illinois Governor J.B. Pritzker posted online graphs and charts to show progress for his state's residents, especially in terms of masks, gloves and other equipment procured.

No matter how well prepared the states were however, a national emergency required federal assistance and states whose governors the President viewed as political opponents or personally disloyal were receiving less aid and getting it later. On March 22, the President complained in a tweet that these states 'shouldn't be blaming others for their shortcomings.' He chided hospitals for their 'insatiable appetite' for supplies. One budget analysis showed that Nebraska with a population of under two million and only 300 coronavirus cases by early April, would receive over $330,000 per patient; New York, with a population of almost 20 million and the highest case load in the US at over 120,000, got a mere $12,000 per sick person.

On April 1, Gov. Pritzker of Illinois warned in a CNN interview of a looming shortage of ventilators as the number of patients soared, while his state had received only ten percent of the masks it needed. Pritzker also estimated Illinois required 4,000 ventilators but had only about 450. New York Governor Andrew Cuomo also told CNN, 'We've gotten about 10% of what we asked for.' *Propublica* reported that the state of New York was paying up to fifteen times the usual price for vital supplies, including $7.50 for paper masks that usually went for under a dollar. When asked at a press conference about Cuomo's comments, the President shot back, 'The problem is, with some people, no matter how much you give it's never enough.'

Washington's Jay Inslee also offended the President. Trump referred to Inslee as a 'snake' who, he later warned would 'take advantage' of federal largesse. In a March 26 teleconference held between the President and a number of governors, Inslee urged the President to use the Defense Production Act to force industry to produce more medical supplies. In a later press briefing where Trump claimed it was a 'great meeting' with 'no contention,' he also snidely referred to Inslee as 'a little wise guy.'

A few days later, as their apparent feud escalated, Trump warned he wished governors would be 'appreciative,' suggesting that their level of deference affected their chances for federal help, and said he wouldn't take calls from governors who 'don't treat you right.' The President had also claimed that governors 'shouldn't be relying on federal government.' The man who publicly refused to take any responsibility also insisted, 'When they disrespect me, they are disrespecting our government, foreshadowing wilder claims of total authority to come.

Michigan racked up nearly 4,700 cases and over a hundred deaths by late March. Trump claimed that he had a 'big problem;' with the 'young, woman governor' in Michigan, complaining that 'all she does is sit there and blame the federal government,' and publicly admitting he had told the Vice President, 'don't call the woman in Michigan.' When New York asked for more equipment, the President was dismissive, **telling Fox's Sean Hannity,** 'I don't believe you need 40,000 or 30,000 ventilators. You know, you go into major hospitals, sometimes they'll have two ventilators. And now all of a sudden they're saying, 'Can we order 30,000 ventilators?'

By mid-April, Unemployment claims had climbed to 22 million in just a few weeks and the Trump's beloved Dow Jones Index remained depressed, having wiped out all the gains it had made since he had taken office. Hospitals were straining under the workload and thousands of healthcare workers had contracted the virus, some fatally. Watching the governor's daily press briefing on TV, the President tweeted on April 18, that Governor Cuomo should 'spend more time doing and less time complaining,' and that he had not been sufficiently thankful for the aid his state had already received.

Rather than get in a similar fight with the President over delays, Maryland ordered half a million test kits directly from South Korea. The administration had stopped a shipment of masks to Canada and the federal authorities were halting supplies to its own hospitals and diverting them to FEMA's stockpiles. Washington's *The Bellingham Herald* reported a shipment of N95 masks for its local hospital and a nearby lab was taken by federal government; The LA Times reported hospitals in several states were not being informed by the feds before the equipment they had ordered was taken. In Illinois, Governor Pritzker's office confirmed it had spent $1.7 million to source medical gear from China and charter flights to ship them in secret, for fear that the government would seize the supplies.

How much help from the federal government a state could expect was becoming increasingly dependent on how much its governor or its voters supported Donald Trump. On April 4, the President had earlier said the federal government was not supposed to act as a 'shipping clerk' for states that he deemed unappreciative. But on April 8, Mr. Trump proudly tweeted, 'Will be immediately sending 100 Ventilators to Colorado at the request of Senator Gardner!' The President was referring to Republican Senator Cory Gardner, even though he had previously denied the same request from the same state's governor Jared Polis, who was a Democrat.

Red States' – those that typically vote Republican and whose governors were firm supporters of Trump – could expect better treatment from the President, or at least, kinder comments. But they also tended to believe his platitudes and were much more relaxed in their coronavirus response. A University of Washington study found that states with Republican governors or high populations of Republicans were slow to adopt social distancing and self-quarantine. Those delays were crucial, potentially allowing hundreds or thousands more infections, depending on activity and population density. The report identified a primary reason for this was cues from the President who 'strongly signaled that the coronavirus was an exaggerated threat or even a hoax – a position that was magnified and reinforced by Republican-leaning media outlets.'

While the White House pandemic specialist Anthony Fauci strongly recommended states issue stay-at-home orders in early April, it remained a suggestion – the federal government could not legally force each state to comply. Some states issued exemptions for hair salons, golf courses and church services, prompting Dr. Fauci to warn during an April 2 press briefing, that social distancing was 'our major weapon against this virus right now. We don't have a vaccine that's deployable. This is the only thing we have.'

Georgia had seen 4,700 cases and over 150 deaths through the month of March, yet schools, shops and cafes; bars and restaurants and fitness centers remained open until Governor Brian Kemp issued a stay-at-home order on April 2. Even Kentucky Senator Rand Paul who had earlier downplayed the dangers posed by the virus, had tested positive but had showed no symptoms. CDC director Robert Redfield explained in a National Public Radio interview, 'We have asymptomatic transmitters and we have individuals who are transmitting 48 hours before they become symptomatic.' Twenty days later, as deaths in Georgia had surged to over 800, Gov. Kemp was still proposing to reopen the state for business.

Florida's Governor Ron DeSantis was another Trump ally who had resisted a lockdown. By early April the state had surged from only a few dozen to over 7,000 cases in just two weeks, yet beaches, resorts and entertainment complexes had remained open, as did church services. On the heels of the new figures the governor was finally compelled to implement stay-at-home orders, but only after thousands of college students had descended on the state for Spring Break festivities, partied hard and then left to all parts of the country.

In states where religious gatherings were exempt from stay-at-home orders, thousands of worshippers crammed into auditoriums to pray away the latest scourge. In March, Virginia Pastor Landon Spradlin drove 900 kilometers south to the New Orleans Mardi Gras where he would preach during festivities while playing the blues with local musicians. Spradlin had decried the media hysteria over Covid-19 as a hoax to undermine President Trump. Spradlin died from coronavirus complications on April 6. Florida Governor Ron DeSantis had declined to bar churches from opening, deeming them an essential service, along with gun stores and WWE wrestling matches. By mid-March, people were even attending 'coronavirus parties,' in order to spread the infection, build 'personal immunity' and give a middle finger to authorities all at once. Kentucky governor Andy Beshear lashed out at such a lightheaded approach in a press conference, saying, 'Anyone who goes to something like this may think they're indestructible, but it's someone else's loved one that they are going to hurt.' Street protests against the economically taxing lockdown orders were organized by right-wing and conservative groups in several states. In the next ten days five states including Oklahoma, Arkansas and Nebraska saw a 50% increase in the rate of infection and South Dakota was up 200%.

In mid-April, with the death toll in the tens of thousands, Rice University found that social distancing was 40% less prevalent in parts of the country that had voted for Donald Trump. Eighteen months and a million deaths later, statistics would show that these areas had been disproportionately affected by their loyalty to Trump. A greater percentage of his supporters were infected and died because they believed the laissez-faire messaging that had filtered down from the top.

Denials and ham-fisted responses continued well into the peak of the pandemic, but even as work on a vaccine was being rushed ahead, Trump continued pandering to religious and fringe factions suspicious of government help, modern medicine and vaccines in general. Once a Covid vaccine became available in late 2020, despite claiming credit for its rollout, Trump initially refused to take a shot. He even later downplayed his own Covid Infection, which turned out to be more serious that initially reported, requiring hospitalization. He famously attended a presidential debate with rival Joe Biden in that election year, when he already knew he was infected. If it was his intention, he failed to make Mr. Biden too sick to run. By late July cases had topped four million, deaths were in five digits. That month Trump assured the public, '99 percent of cases are totally harmless,' despite the hospitalization rate being much higher than 1%. By mid-year several major news networks had stopped airing the White House's daily Covid briefings for fear of spreading misinformation dangerous to public health.

Among Trump's wilder assertions during 2020 were two instances where he suggested miracle cures, one already popular on the fringe and another pulled directly out of his own ass. Both of these led to further health crises and avoidable deaths. In April, sharing the podium with one of his public health experts

Deborah Birx, Trump noted the effectiveness of household cleaners such as bleach in killing the virus on surfaces, and openly wondered if there was some way to inject such a treatment into the human bloodstream. 'It'd be interesting to check,' Mr. Trump said in front of the cameras as a noticeably surprised Dr Birx shuffled uncomfortably beside him. He was also impressed by the use of ultra-violet light, again on surfaces, and suggested, we hit the body with a tremendous—whether it's ultraviolet or just very powerful light ... supposing you brought the light inside of the body, which you can do either through the skin or in some other way,' earning an all-too-mild rebuke from the stunned Dr Birx.

Subsequently, various state health departments reported a spike in calls asking whether it was safe to ingest Clorox or alcohol cleaning products. New York. Michigan Tennessee and Illinois all reported an uptick in calls to poison control centers and some also reported medical callouts and emergency room visits after people used detergents for sinus rinses or gargled bleach. Kansas even re[ported one case of a man who drank bleach. When Trump was asked about people using disinfectant in light of his comments his response was, 'I can't imagine why.' Asked whether he accepted any responsibility, Trump again stated, 'No, I don't.'

By the time vaccines rolled out late in 2020, fringe websites, the religious right and conspiracy theorists were uniting in their distrust of large pharmaceutical companies directed by governments to deliver compulsory shots. A popular theory circulating the internet in right wing circles was the use of hydroxychloroquine – a malaria drug. The FDA had originally allowed emergency use of the drug – which like bleach by the way, contained chlorine molecules, but revoked this authorization shortly after when it showed no discernible result in hospitalized Covid-19 patients. With side effects such as heart arrhythmia its benefits did not outweigh known and potential risks. Nevertheless Trump publicly promoted the drug, touting it in press conferences and on line tweets. As early as May 2020, he had claimed he was using hydroxychloroquine as a preventive. Even in Late July after studies had debunked its efficacy, Trump still exhorted followers to try the drug, saying, 'I happen to believe in it. I would take it. As you know, I took it for a 14-day period. And as you know, I'm here. I happen to think it works in the early stages' Use caught on for a time at home and abroad and the speculative use of hydroxychloroquine for COVID-19 threatened its availability for malaria treatment throughout the year 2020.

The next shiny object was Ivermectin, an anti-parasitic drug used to treat river blindness, scabies and head lice in humans and parasitic worms in horses. Again, some research had suggested efficacy against Covid-19 in lab tests but there was no delivery system such as pills or shots approved for human delivery. Moreover the studies later proved faulty, misleading or downright fraudulent. The main reason for the theory's continued popularity was that it was an alternative to injected vaccinations and because it came out of the internet and circulated among communities of the suspicious-minded. Partly because of his own gullibility and partly due to his canny sense of appeal to these fringes, Donald Trump was quick to endorse the horse drug,

The misinformation stemmed from the drug's base ingredient, not the Equine dewormer's off the shelf product. Nevertheless, the faithful continued to purchase and consume the veterinary drug, causing shortages and enduring unnecessary side effects (when applied for head lice the drug effectively poisons the patient's blood, and therefore the food supply for the parasites). As with the previous miracle drug, Poison control centers across the country saw a dramatic surge in calls from people self-medicating with Ivermectin. Many of these cases stemmed from people ingesting the veterinary drug instead of its cousin intended for human use. Nebraska alone saw over a thousand overdose cases in 2021, a 163% increase over the previous year. Two more Trump states – Minnesota and Kentucky also reported spikes. In Kentucky only a quarter of the exposure cases were from people who had a prescription: 75% had bought the dewormer from farming suppliers or feed stores. Worse still, the missed opportunity inherent in self-medicating caused many to get sick, or sicker than they needed to from Covid, potentially causing more hospitalizations and deaths.

None of these wonder cures had any genuine clinical impact on the disease despite being promoted by Trump and his surrogates. Trump continued to deny the seriousness of the pandemic well into the election season. On October 29, a week before the election, he stated, 'Well, why aren't they talking about deaths? Oh, oh, because the number is almost nothing. Because we've gotten control of this, and we understand how it works.' Team Trump continued to discourage masks, social distancing and vaccination, though he attempted to take credit for the vaccine's development. This came at a time when 1,000 people were dying every day from the disease. When challenged by one reporter on the hideous death toll, Trump quipped, 'It is what it is.'

This nonchalance may well have contributed to Trump's election loss in November of 2020. The resulting economic shock was felt as deeply as the shock of seeing all those hazard suits, body bags and overflowing hospital morgues. By the time Trump left office in early 2021, Covid-19 deaths in the United States were nearing a million, while studies showed that over 300,000 of those could have been prevented if it were not for delays and disinformation – especially over vaccines. Whereas European and Asian leaders had closed borders, maintained curfews and mobilized national health apparatuses, the 45th President laid the foundations for a crisis, ignored the looming crisis, denied it was a crisis, responded slowly to the crisis and finally acted mostly in his own political interests rather than those of the nation. This cost hundreds of thousands more lives than would have been likely had the response been firmer. When faced with questions of why his administration had been so slow to react he responded with more denial, finger-pointing and scapegoating. Promoting a slew of snake-oil remedies and fake cures, and denying proven scientific and medical advice, the misinformation spread by the President himself caused hundreds of thousands of unnecessary deaths.

While the Covid-19 debacle most likely cost Trump the presidency, he was not content to merely kill by neglect. There was one more spasm of violence left to commit in the president's final days in office. Refusing to concede defeat to Joe Biden after November 2020 election, Trump and his legal and media teams, as well as hangers-on and fellow travelers in congress and TV punditry, set about on a grand scheme to deceive the American public and have the election signed back over to him. This attempted coup will be outlined in more detail in Chapter 8: Thou Shalt Not Steal. When it looked like this plan was failing however, and congress was about to certify the election win On January 6th 2021, Trump had one more ace up his sleeve – to attempt a violent takeover.

As congress met to certify the results – a necessary final step before the peaceful handover of power on January 20, Trump gathered an ever-growing crowd of supporters in front of

Capitol Hill in Washington DC. Mostly white working lass men, the thousands of faithful had travelled from all over the country to rally in support of the President's claim the election had been 'stolen' or 'rigged'. Trump had spent the past two months on twitter, on TV, in speeches and other media, firing up his political base and convincing them that Democrats had cast millions of fake votes, cheated in the count and used other nefarious means to ensure Trump would lose. Now, on the day that the results tallied by each state were to be submitted and formalized – with Trump's Vice President Mike Pence presiding – an army of disgruntled fans assembled outside.

They came from a motley assortment from unemployed to self employed. Though most were barely high school graduates, some were doctors and lawyers. Again most were white, most over thirty and from Trump states and counties that had expected him to win. There were survivalists and libertarians; neo-confederates waving Dixie flags, Incels and conspiracy theorists; ex-cops and a lot of ex-cons. Some were former or even active duty military personnel. Some associated themselves with various right-wing militia groups such as the Proud Boys, Oath Keepers and Three-Percenters. Many subscribed conspiracy themed websites such as QAnon. Trump had previously told these groups to 'stand back and stand by' in support of his causes. Some had come to set things right as they saw it, many had come to start a revolution or the 'Second Civil War' that remains a popular fantasy on neo-nationalist websites. Apart from a few in wild costumes, such as the notorious QAnon Shaman, shirtless, tattooed and draped in animal furs, most wore Trump hats and Trump T-shirts, waved Trump banners and Trump flags and were there to support Trump's bid to hold on to the presidency after losing a free and fair election.

Trump stood behind a bulletproof glass shield on a pulpit that chilly January morning and told his crowd of faithful that his Vice President Pence had better 'do the right thing' and that they should 'fight like hell or you're not gonna have a country left.' He implored upon them to march on the Capitol, promising he would be 'right beside' them. As proceedings continued inside the congress, state electors submitting their votes and the vice president formally tallying them, the crowd outside became more agitated and drew closer. The results of the election were already in and the number of states that had gone for each candidate were well known so the certification was just the final formality. Everyone expected Mike Pence to declare Trump's opponent the lawful winner. Some of the crowd were chanting that Mike Pence should be hanged and a symbolic gallows was hoisted above the crowd amidst the fluttering Trump campaign flags and other paraphernalia.

Trump left for his White House bunker as the marchers shuffled on toward congress becoming more agitated with each step. He would not be marching with them that day or participating in the riot that he had set up. Instead he continued to tweet his support as the afternoon darkened and his most motivated foot soldiers began to test the police barriers and cordons around the building. Riot shields and batons clashed as the day wore on, bottles, bricks and Molotov cocktails were hurled. They carried baseball bats, flagpoles, knuckle dusters and other melee weapons. They fought their way through several barricades, stomping and beating police officers, smashing windows and breaching doors as teargas coiled in the air around them.

Congressmen fled through the back doors, or into safe rooms. Mike Pence was hustled away through a tunnel by the secret service and driven off. The scene looked like the final evacuation of the US Embassy in Saigon, minus the helicopters. When they finally got inside, the offenders vandalized and looted. Men were filmed urinating on the walls, carrying off embossed lecterns or office equipment such as laptop computers. One was said to have defecated in the halls. Some were filmed with heavy tape and ropes and handcuffs among other weapons – intending to capture the vice president or members of congress they had a beef with. The battle raged on until early evening when finding nothing, and facing a pushback from reinforced police presence, the rioters fled or were arrested.

The final death toll on the day was only five – a handful of police and one or two of the rioters. However hundreds were wounded and some officers suffered life-changing injuries and had to quit the force. Because all of this was caught on news cameras and CCTV, identifications came thick and fast.

Hundreds of rioters were rounded up across the country and duly charged. Some went into hiding and the hunt continues for them today. In subsequent charges it was found the leaders of groups such as the Proud Boys and Oath Keepers had stashed firearms and were intending to sue the riot to stage a violent government takeover - their leaders were subsequently handed long sentences. However the blame for those deaths and injuries surely falls on Trump's shoulders. He threatened the lives of congressmen – many in his own party; sent a mob to trash the seat of peaceful governance in the United States and even set his minions up to hang the vice president – if they caught him.

If Trump was indirectly, but very clearly responsibly for excess pandemic deaths, his direct and willful call to violence led to several deaths on January 6 – and all to stop the peaceful transfer of power after he lost an election. His spree did not end with an election loss either. As outlined in Chapter Nine, Trump has continued to peddle the lie that the election was stolen, causing state and county officials in areas of Michigan, Georgia and Arizona that saw narrow contests, to receive death threats and worse from local Trump fans. Some had to take on police protection and others had to move house altogether. Continuing the campaign of intimidation, when Trump's criminal trials finally kicked off in the state of New York, he was accused of witness tampering, threatening judges and their family members and finally slapped with a gag order. He has used this tactic in challenges against his election losses, trials for bank fraud and campaign finance violations in New York, and even against election officials and other public officers for pure revenge. Trump knows that he need only say a name and point a finger and some armed crazy will do his bidding. Reuters offered a deep dive in early 2024 into the numerous instances of resulting threats and harassment across his many trials and documented over 27,000 threats against Judges and prosecutors in the years since his election loss.

These crazies may yet the shock troops of a future Trump administration. Recalling his dog-whistle encouragement of the proud bys, in June of 2024 amid his latest presidential run he referred to the rioters of January 6th as 'warriors' and dangled pardons for the many who were convicted should he become president. His campaign also promised an army of 'foot soldiers' to act as poll watchers – ostensibly to watch for irregularities but in reality to intimidate and discourage anyone who might vote for the opposition. Violence has been part and parcel of the Trump presidential ethos from day one and only showed signs of worsening if he should win again in 2024.

7.   THOU SHALT NOT COMMIT ADULTERY

'I just start kissing them. I don't even wait. When you're a star, they let you do it, you can do anything. Grab 'em by the pussy. You can do anything.'

- Mulligans, 3:41

The President of the United States has been married three times. He cheated on his first wife with his second and his second with his third; his third with a Playboy model and an adult film actress (These are just the two mistresses we know of so far) and one of these while his third wife was still nursing his fifth child. Keeping up? To put it bluntly, Donald J. Trump fucks around.

His affairs are not the worst of it. He has been accused and even boasted of committing sexual assault; was filmed creeping on teenage and pre-pubescent girls and has joked about having a carnal interest in his own daughter. So how did the religious right get to throw its considerable (and sanctimonious) weight behind a serial adulterer and cheat, womanizer, groper and alleged rapist? Well, they never liked women much anyway. Their book does exhort them to 'be fruitful and multiply' (Genesis 9:7), which Trump appears to be aptly attempting.

Like many rich boys, he was known in his youth as a bit of a player, and it seems that like many sociopaths he was able to feign charm before the obvious creeping dementia took hold in later years. Watch an interview with Trump from the eighties and he can scarcely be the same man – except for the toupee and the obvious narcissism. A forty-year-old Donald Trump was lucid, charming and quick with one-liners; he seemed to know his business at the time, which was the New York real estate market. He was just as shameless a self-promoter but a much cannier and more convincing one. Still, it is not hard to see how this, coupled with the wealth, business reputation and the trappings of success he enjoyed, would draw a certain type of woman to him.

That type was apparently Eastern European models in search of a rich husband and permanent residency. The first was Ivana Trump, a Czechoslovakian model and businesswoman who had emigrated to the US. Ivana had a history both before of latching onto wealthy, powerful men and The Donald was no exception. They were married in 1977 and she bore his three older children, Don Junior, Eric and de-facto Secretary of State and renowned shoe saleswoman Ivanka. The marriage ended acrimoniously in 1990 amid allegations of marital abuse and even rape, though these complaints were withdrawn and Ivana settled for a shit-ton of cash instead. By then Trump had already been banging his next wife for some time.

Marla Maples was an actress best known for B-movies and winning beauty pageants in both her home state of Georgia and in Hawaii. Younger, prettier, just as blonde as Ivana, she mothered Trump's fourth child, the tearaway Tiffany who rarely sees much of the limelight compared to Trump's other children. The New York Post, a tabloid paper and frequent Trump cheerleader, once claimed in a headline Maples had called sex with Trump the best she'd ever had. It was apparently not enough to stop her getting some elsewhere as the couple eventually divorced amid allegations she was having an affair with her bodyguard. It later came out in Trump's campaign finance trial that he had an arrangement with the *Post's* publishers to invent stories that put him in a good light.

Not surprisingly, Trump's third wife Melania Knauss was also a model, this time Slovenian and again younger than the previous, even as Trump himself was well into his fifties. They began dating as usual, while he was still married. The couple waited some years after his second divorce in 1999 and finally wed in 2005. Incidentally his later political rivals the Clintons were in attendance and the guests were entertained ironically with a new version of the Jazz standard, The Lady is a Tramp. A year later Donald and Melania were blessed with their first son together and Trump's fifth child, the surly, slack-jawed Barron. This name, it should be noted, is the same as the pseudonym used by Trump when he posed as a PR man in his earlier attempts to court the press. Perhaps The Don has only a few names up his sleeve; perhaps he always liked that one; maybe he was just taking the piss.

It came to light during the Trump presidency that Trump was having affairs even when Melania had just given birth to their son. It was known to some during his campaign but using a tabloid media technique called catch-and-kill, or 'spiking' a story, a friendly paper *The National Inquirer* paid one of these mistresses for tell-all rights then never published the stories. Now legally bound to silence and with the only people who knew being loyal to Trump, the secret would be safe. Except for crimes committed in the act.

Now while many might be put off by Trump having extramarital affairs – or even the caliber of women he chose to do so with – the purpose of this book is not to moralize over someone's personal life. No law was broken when he slept with someone else, and personally, it's no skin off my nose. But the evangelicals who so staunchly support Trump and claim to promote 'family values' (usually just code for hating gays and stopping everyone else having fun) should have taken greater issue with his conduct. Instead, you could hear the crickets, even in winter.

The first of the relevant trysts was with a pornographic film performer whose stage name was Stormy Daniels. They spent the night together at one of Trump's golf resorts in 2006. Unlike his former wife allegedly did, Stormy gave a less-than-gushing review about both The Donald's size and his performance that evening. The second was a playboy model Karen McDougal whom he dated later that year. It was McDougal whom *The National Inquirer* later paid $150,000 then buried the story, as revealed in Trump's 2024 hush money trial.

The now infamous *Access Hollywood* tape released during the 2016 campaign, in which Trump can be heard boasting of forcing women to kiss him and groping their genitals, uses his own words succinctly. In a moment during the interview with a radio shock jock when he thinks the microphones are turned off, Trump brags that 'When you're a star, they let you do anything…you can grab 'em by the pussy.' The tape also features Trump relating the story of a time he tried (and failed) to seduce another married celebrity by taking her furniture shopping. 'I moved on her like a bitch,' he joked, in a rare self-deprecating moment. The tape is dated around the same time as the affairs, in late 2005. That's at least three real or attempted affairs during the time his wife was pregnant or had recently given birth. Still, crickets.

Yet while the act itself of sleeping with a porn star may not be illegal, the effort to silence her fell afoul of campaign finance laws. In 2016, ten years after the night at the resort, Donald Trump's lawyer and fixer, Michael Cohen facilitated a $130,000 hush-money payment to Stormy Daniels. This payment was never disclosed in expense declarations and the Trump team at one point claimed it was merely a personal agreement, which would not be illegal. However, a New York federal court successfully demonstrated that because the payment had been made during the campaign and the woman's silence would have been beneficial to Trump's candidacy, it was indeed an 'in-kind campaign contribution' to the campaign: money spent for the purposes of the election. Cohen pleaded guilty and went to prison; Trump remained a co-conspirator in court records, effectively a de facto conviction in itself, and potentially a problem after his term was up and he leaves the protection of the office of President.

The crickets continued to chirp until 2023. Having gathered enough evidence including financial records and Cohen's conviction and testimony, the Manhattan DA pounced. Trump made history by becoming the first president – sitting or former – to be slapped with a criminal indictment. The charges sprang from the falsification of business records in which Donald Trump, his accountants and lawyers wrote of the hush-money payments as vague 'legal expenses.' The prosecutors charged that Trump had knowingly arranged to have Ms Daniels paid off ten years after the affair and during an election campaign in order to conceal this inconvenient voters from his presumably conservative-leaning voters. They identified 3 separate acts of falsifying checks that were then passed on to Mr Cohen who had paid Ms Daniels out of his own pocket.

Normally this falsification would be a misdemeanor, but the prosecution argued that because it was committed in the furtherance of another crime – concealing information from the voters in an election year and hiding payments that amounted to in-kind campaign contributions – that under new York statutes this elevated the offence to a felony. This was potentially punishable by prison time.

The Trump legal team claimed variously that it was true that these were unrelated expenses, that he had never had sex with Stormy Daniels, that the payments were to conceal the affair from his wife Melania, and that since he was a sitting President at the time he wrote some of the checks, he was protected by 'executive privilege.' Since Cohen had already been convicted to doing this on Trump's behalf and he was most certainly no longer president it was a weak defense. Likewise the claim he only wanted to conceal accusations of infidelity from his wife: the payments took place in 2016 during Trump's first presidential run and a decade after the affair.

The trial was held in New York City in the spring of 2024 and featured among other things, the sight of the 78-year-old former president looking deflated and sometimes nodding off during proceedings. Because he still even denied the affair had taken place, Trump was treated to Ms Daniel's testimony regarding his disappointing performance in bed and Mr Cohen laying bare in front of his face all the crimes they had committed together. In the end the jury found him guilty on all 34 counts, making history again as Trump became the first former president turned convicted felon.

The sleaze neither begins nor ends at Trump's affairs, however. He has shown an unhealthy interest in underage girls and a propensity towards sexual assault as well. In one famous video he chats up a pre-teen girl on the escalators of Trump Tower, telling the reporter with him 'I'm gonna be dating her in ten years.' In another incident, he is alleged to have told a pair of fourteen-year-old beauty pageant contestants he'd be dating them 'in a couple of years,' which still wouldn't be legal. Other teen pageant contestants have alleged Trump used to enter their changing rooms unannounced and conduct 'inspections.' One model quoted in Barry Levine and Monique El-Faizy's book All the President's Women which details many more such predatory accounts, recalled, 'I remember him saying: 'Oh, how old are you?' And I said seventeen, and he said, 'That's just great; you're not too old, not too young.'' Legally, she was too young.

Not surprising then, is the president's long association with convicted child sex trafficker Jeffrey Epstein. Trump was in attendance at many celebrity parties entertained by underage models in the eighties and nineties as detailed in Levine and El-Faizy, and perhaps it was at one of these the two became acquainted. Trump famously gushed that his friend Epstein a billionaire hedge fund manager and financier, also had a taste for beautiful women and that 'many of them' were 'on the younger side'. Trump spent a lot of time partying and golfing with

Epstein, visiting his private Caribbean island on a corporate jet that was known locally as the Lolita Express (flight logs show Trump boarded the aircraft at least seven times). In one famous video can be seen entertaining Epstein at a party full of models and cheerleaders, egging him on and leering at young women.

While the political Right has enjoyed playing up the few occasions when other rich and powerful people such as the Clintons met Epstein, they are curiously silent about the many occasions he partied with Donald J Trump. When Epstein strangled himself in his cell while awaiting sentencing, the Right-wing propaganda machine and an army of internet trolls merely added him to the apocryphal Clinton Body Count, an alleged list of assassinations committed by Bill and Hillary to shore up their political careers and bury damaging associations. Yet Trump must surely have known of Epstein's proclivities. In one now-famous recorded interview from the early 2000's, Trump can be heard singing Epstein's praises, remarking 'He's a lot of fun to be with. It is even said that he likes beautiful women as much as I do, and many of them are on the younger side.'

The religious Right has a curious attitude towards underage sex. On the one hand, pre-marital sex is forbidden and the pursuit of girls below eighteen a stick to beat foreigners and Muslims with whenever the subject of child brides comes up. On the other hand, they just loves them some jailbait. Southern Republican states have the highest rates of teenage pregnancies, the lowest ages for marital consent (with the parents' permission of course) and the highest number of child brides in the United States. It should come as no surprise that a Republican Senate candidate in Alabama, Roy Moore whom many women accused of sexual assault when they were minors in the seventies and eighties, received the blessings of both the evangelical community and Donald Trump. Alabama State Auditor Jim Zeigler – a Republican of course – explained it neatly for us: '...take Joseph and Mary. Mary was a teenager and Joseph was an adult carpenter. They became parents of Jesus.' Moore lost his race, but not by much. He later expressed interest in running for governor.

One of the more common defenses of Trump is that actions and words are different, dismissing some of his creepier statements as 'locker room talk' or for the religiously inclined, instructive flaws bestowed on him from above. Yet Trump seems equally a man of action when it comes to his own descriptions of the way he sexually assaults women, and actions do indeed speak louder than words. Dozens of women from Trump's past have come out with allegations of touching, groping, forced kisses and attempted rape since he announced his candidacy and the list has grown throughout his presidency. This far surpasses the number mustered by any of his predecessors. Another roundup is in order.

Donald Trump's sexual misconduct allegations are so numerous as to warrant their own Wiki page. Bill Clinton is the only other president to have achieved this. Not only did Trump's first wife initially allege marital rape; several employees have sued him for harassment, including in 2017, Summer Zervos from his TV show The Apprentice, and businesswoman Jill Harth twenty years earlier. After the 2016 leak of the by then decade-old Access Hollywood tape, a flood of accusers materialized. In fact close to two dozen women have come forward, including the aforementioned pageant contestants, with allegations ranging from leering to touching to penetration itself.

Jill Harth claimed Trump placed his hands between her legs at dinner, as well as pushing her against the wall and forcing a kiss; a campaign staffer claimed he had forcibly kissed her as well at a Florida rally; Businesswoman Jessica Leeds claimed Trump fondled her on a flight across the country; aspiring model Kristin Anderson said he groped her at a nightclub; Cathy Heller was allegedly groped and kissed at Trump's Mar-a-Lago resort; a former Miss Utah contestant has similar tales of grabbing and groping; Journalist Natasha Stoynoff recalls a forced kiss and on it goes, with over twenty such women coming forward. One accuser whose name was suppressed but later withdrew her charges for fear of death threats from Trump's rabid fan base claimed at an Epstein-hosted party in the early nineties when she was only thirteen she was raped by Donald Trump.

The best-verified is the claim by fashion writer E. Jean Carroll that Trump raped her in a department store changing room in the nineties. As of early 2020, a New York judge had ruled against Trump is his efforts to stop a civil case for defamation stemming from this alleged assault. Trump was found guilty of said defamation in 2023 and forced to pay compensation Ms Carroll. Because a civil jury found that Carroll cannot have been lying and therefore that Trump's subsequent attacks on her character constitute defamation, this also makes Trump now legally recognized as Carroll's attacker. The court awarded her $83 million in damages in the civil case.

For the most part, Donald Trump has proven to be publicly proud of his sexual misadventures. When challenged by some of his accusers he would sometimes dismiss them as not attractive enough for him to bother assaulting, both a callous deflection and a suggestion that he'd have a go if only they were prettier. Neither helps his case. He has boasted of being popular with women, bragged about the ease with which he believes his fame lets him get away with groping people and posed as a PR insider when calling into radio shows and newspapers to spill the 'gossip' on his relationships. His most lurid recording, in which he told a TV host he would happily force kisses and grab women's genitals uninvited, was considerably better received by evangelicals than their otherwise prudish credentials would indicate they'd accept. Never mind that this neatly corroborates the M.O. described by his many accusers. Never mind that the story broke on the eve of an election: Trump still carried the evangelical vote by over eighty percent.

Mr Trump's history of boasting about sex goes back much further than his candidacy. He once told an interviewer that, in lieu of committing to military service like many young men of his generation, the dating scene of the nineteen-seventies was his 'personal Vietnam' in which he avoided the minefield of STDS and other apparent dangers. Way to support the troops, Donald.

Many years before becoming president, he bragged to shock jock Howard Stern on his radio program about walking in on his pageant contestants, corroborating their allegations in advance: 'No men are anywhere, and I'm allowed to go in because I'm the owner of the pageant and therefore I'm inspecting it...and you see these incredible looking women, and so I sort of get away with things like that.' A contestant later explained that had made her feel, 'the dirtiest I felt in my entire life'.

Under guises and names like John Barron and John Miller – a fictional Trump insider or publicist – Trump called in to reporters and claimed that he had been pursued by Madonna among other celebrities. This was, of course, wishful thinking, but also a lie about his appeal to improve his standing. The first pseudonym, Barron was conceived as early as 1980 and used throughout the proceeding decade to speak for Trump whenever he wanted to make himself look good. He used the identity to inflate his assets in communications with Forbes Magazine, getting onto its rich list and using that reputation to secure further bank loans. The nickname was retired when Trump was compelled to admit in court he'd made the character up. Caveat emptor.

The second, John Miller, was used to talk up the real estate mogul's popularity with women during his first highly public divorce in the early nineties; it was then that the claim was made he had been approached by Madonna seeking a date. Yes, apparently the biggest pop star in the world at the time needed a date with an aging, toupee-wearing, pudgy self-styled billionaire. Some of his followers no doubt still believe it. To back up his claims of success with women, a subsequent female secretary was also invented who wrote, 'I do not believe any man in America gets more calls from women wanting to see him, meet him, or go out with him. The most beautiful women, the most successful women—all women love Donald Trump.'

This pattern of repetition and hyperbole closely resembles Trump's signature speaking and tweeting style, as does the sheer amount of bullshit. Now that Trump's voice is so familiar, the recordings that exist of the call-ins leave no doubt it was Donald Trump on the line.

The reaction from Trump's religious base to all these sexual shenanigans has been mostly muted: The publication *Christianity Today*, started by the late mega-church huckster and second-rate Jesus salesman Billy Graham has been rather muted on Trump's adulterousness. In late 2019, the magazine's editor Mark Galli upbraided the president on the political skullduggery that led to his impeachment (courageously, a few days before retiring) and received the usual nasty tweets from the president and a public evangelical backlash including from the Reverend

Graham's son and third-rate Jesus salesman, Franklin. However, Galli had little to say on the affairs aside from expressing mild disapproval and noting many evangelicals liken Trump to the biblical King David, also a notorious womanizer whom God punished – but allowed to remain king.

Other evangelical leaders had similar excuses for their relative silence on Trump's promiscuity.   Perhaps because they're in the same business: the Texas paper Forth Worth Star-Telegram uncovered hundreds of accusations of sex abuse against dozens of fundamentalist pastors. Some quote Romans 3:23, which laments that everyone is a sinner. It seems almost every other week a Baptist or Pentecostal minister or one of those ghastly 'prosperity gospel' conmen proves the Bible right; being caught with a mistress, a love child, a gay escort or all three, with drugs on the motel room coffee table.

Others, simply accept a certain amount of sexual predation as natural, even 'biblical.' When Alabama Senate Candidate Roy Moore was credibly accused of assaulting several underage girls during his career, far from being chased out of the state, he lost by only a narrow margin. Supporters cited underage marriage in the Bible as a defense. Florida congressman and prominent Trump supporter Matt Gaetz came under investigation in 2024 for allegedly attending cocaine-fueled orgies with girls under eighteen; the same year Trump spiritual advisor Robert Morris resigned from his post as senior pastor at a Texas mega church (where else?) after admitting he molested a twelve-year-old many years prior. New Hampshire Republican senator Jess Edwards argued against raising the legal age of marriage to eighteen because young girls are 'ripe and fertile'. Republican-led states lead the nation in child-marriage and teen pregnancies.

While many of the same religious figures and sanctimonious politicians heartily condemned Bill Clinton for his sexual improprieties they have not applied the same standard to Donald Trump, partly because he allows their fundamentalist agenda to have its day in court by appointing Christian conservative judges to the federal benches and Supreme Court. When asked about the president's known affair with the porn star Stormy Daniels, head of the Family Research Council Tony Perkins used the kind of golfing analogy that resonates with entitled old white men: 'All right, you get a Mulligan, you get a do-over here.'

A reputed cheat at golf as well, Mr. Trump will no doubt take Perkins up on the offer sooner or later.

8.   THOU SHALT NOT STEAL

'I just need you to find 11,780 votes...'

-   Conspiracies, 2:23

Brace yourselves because this is going to be a long one. Donald J. Trump is a crook. This cannot be said enough. Not only is he a crook, most of his kids are crooks because that's how he has taught them to do business – those who work anyway; Christ alone knows what Tiffany does. His youngest son will probably turn out to be a crook one day too, if he doesn't just coast along like his half-sister.

If that sounds too mean, I'm surprised you've read this far. They're all crooks: tax-dodging, payment-avoiding, bill-stiffing, self-dealing, charity-fleecing con-artists and fraudsters, and they have collectively at Donald Trump's behest and under his leadership taken Trump supporters for a jolly old ride. Furthermore, Trump has admitted his criminality so many times – in political debates, court proceedings, legal settlements and on live TV – that even his evangelical supporters cannot have failed to notice, despite closing their eyes, covering their ears and stomping and screaming they don't want to hear about it. It has been normalized.

Since the start of his business career, Trump has looked for shortcuts. Some of the tricks he learned from his father as a real estate developer in New York. One of their favorites was to ensure lower property taxes by undervaluing the properties. This is called tax fraud. Another trick was overvaluing the properties for the purpose of insurance or as collateral for bank loans: insurance fraud and bank fraud. Trump the businessman remains under indictment and on trial by prosecutors in New York for these.

He has been sued no less than 1,400 times, including class actions against his organization and his person. These include defamation, harassment, more than 100 tax disputes. This, his defenders claim, is a natural part of doing business, but the volume of litigation surrounding Trump has been anything but normal. He was first sued in 1973 by the Justice Department (which as president over forty years later, he has conveniently stuffed with yes-men). This was for violations of the Fair Housing Act in which his residential apartment buildings denied potential black tenants in favor of white ones. We'll call this stealing housing opportunities from minorities. He was forced to settle in 1975 but was back in court three years later for breaching the settlement: stealing from the needy again. In the 1980s he stole from the poor once more, using underhand tactics to force tenants out of his buildings, so he could demolish them and make more money on new ones. The court eventually forced him to leave the buildings alone.

In 1988 he was sued by the government again, this time for violating antitrust laws: misreporting public information related to a stock purchase: stealing from clients. His casinos were fined in the nineties for removing employees of color: stealing jobs. His father once bought over three million dollars in chips from an Atlantic City casino to circumvent inheritance laws; stealing from the tax man again. He was later in court for misreporting earnings from casinos. When a real estate deal fell through in 2004 his investors and developers sued for fraud. He has also been sued by contractors for work completed but that he refused to pay for claiming it was unsatisfactory. To summarize, Trump is a man who cheats when he can and avoids paying his bills at all costs.

One of Trump's better cons was pulled off in the early eighties and may have facilitated much of the business he has done over the past few decades. It is also likely to become part of a brewing case in the federal courts over Trump's tax returns and business dealings in New York. Using his pseudonyms he contacted reporters at Forbes magazine, a monthly circle-jerk for the wealthy and connected, claiming to have knowledge of Trump's high net worth. He claimed at the time he was worth $400 million when it is estimated by others that aside from his still-living father's assets, Trump was personally only worth about a tenth of that at the time. Never one to lie small, The

Donald convinced the publication that he belonged on their rich list and then used that reputation to secure huge loans for future ventures. He has since defaulted with and been sued by so many large domestic and international banks most no longer do business with his organizations, sparking speculation he has had to turn to Russian oligarchs via Deutsche Bank for easy cash. The investigation is ongoing. Trump himself has boasted of being called 'The King of Debt'.

In a 2016 election debate against opponent Hillary Clinton, he was reminded that he had avoided paying taxes for years, to which he responded, 'Because I'm smart.' That moment may have been one of the triggers for authorities to look deeper into the candidate's tax returns. The New York District attorney, federal Southern District of New York and congressional committees would all eventually begin to examine Trump's dealings.

As a man most banks would no longer do business with, where did his loans come from? For a businessman with a long history and such vaunted wealth, why had he managed to write off a billion dollars in losses and avoid paying tax for a decade? As a candidate Trump promised to be transparent and release his tax returns, as most past presidents have done for forty years; as President, he has litigated tooth and nail to keep these records not just hidden from the public, but out of the hands of the authorities.

As summarized by Kenneth Boyd of the CPA institute, in 1979 Trump took multi-million dollar 'loans' from his father with no repayment schedule or interest. Investigators now argue these were gifts and should have been taxed as such. A couple of years later when he inherited $90 million worth of property from a dead relative, his organization valued these at only $13 million in order to pay a lower estate tax, an act of appraisal fraud he and his siblings similarly committed when they inherited their father's properties two decades later. A decade later Trump committed securities and loan fraud, 'buying back' shares sold to his father for a fraction of their value and as mentioned, 'selling' over $3 million in casino chips that were never used. He also engaged in inflating expense reports at businesses owned, another ploy to avoid paying higher taxes. The man's career has been a litany of fraud case, avoiding paying his fair share of taxes while the chumps who support him pride themselves on being upstanding, honest citizens.

This is stealing from the public coffers. If it takes a village to raise a child, it takes a nation to raise a billionaire. Tax dollars go into education, roads, bridges, rail, Medicare, Medicaid, the military; veterans, welfare programs, the police, courts, lawmaking, and public administration − the infrastructure that supports and protects businesses and allows capital to be applied and to grow. Rich men should feel obligated to pay society back for facilitating their wealth, the way Bill Gates, George Soros, Mark Cuban, Warren Buffet and other real billionaires do.

Instead, Trump takes pride in dodging this responsibility because he's 'smart'.

It is not just the government Trump has short-changed. The list of organizations, banks, individuals that no longer do business with Trump because he doesn't pay is as long as his whole career. While his supporters extol the virtues of free enterprise and private capital, Trump has done his share of not paying for services rendered. It came to light in the 2016 campaign that Trump never misses an opportunity to stiff the average Joe either. A cabinetmaking contractor ended up going out of business after completing a $400,000 job at one casino that it was never paid for. Trump companies have been sued for failing to pay workers overtime; carpenters, engineers, electricians, lighting and air conditioning installers; over 250 contractors not paid, not paid in full or not paid on time for work done at Trump properties. Most of these were small businesses that could ill afford the loss, or to be tied up in litigation chasing Trump up for the money. Most had to write it off; not a few were forced out of business.

We've already heard how Trump has nudged people of color out of employment at his casinos. At his gold clubs and resorts and wineries, there has been a pattern of minority exploitation as well. While Trump the candidate railed against illegal immigration, Trump the businessman at the same time employed undocumented workers as cooks, cleaners, grape pickers, construction workers and groundsmen. These were often summarily dismissed at the season's end, sometimes without pay. Well into his presidency, the Washington Post was still uncovering multiple cases of undocumented workers at Trump properties and businesses, some no doubt serving him and his cabinet as they plotted to deport their families. Often when the heat was on, managers would quickly dismiss the workers, but this only prompted them to go to reporters and expose the situation. In this neat little twofer, Trump has managed to stiff to groups; migrant laborers and his supporters who believe he's serious about stopping them. Only the former deserves any sympathy.

And the latter? Trump has a long history of fleecing those who have bought into him as well. Some of these are innocent victims, many are willing enablers. All have been proven suckers for trusting him. If you have ever believed in Trump the brand, if you've bought his books, paid for his advice, or voted for his policies, he has taken you for a fool as well.

First his readers. Trump has published half a dozen ghost-written books on success and getting rich. The problem is he never *got* rich; he was *born* rich. He claims to be worth ten billion dollars, but some experts place estimates as low as $400 million – today's equivalent more or less of what he has inherited from his family, making it quite possible Trump has never actually *made* a net dollar. His forays into actual business have ended in disaster: Trump Airlines, Trump Steaks, Trump Casinos, all kaput. He sold his readers on the myth of the self-made man when he'd lost far more money than he had ever made, and only managed to hold onto his inheritance because it is tied up in real estate. The only 'business' he has had any luck in is branding – selling his name to others to put on their buildings, and even that has taken a hit since the public bigotry, misogyny and racism surrounding his political career have made his name much less marketable.

In the meantime, Trump has filed for almost as many bankruptcies as success-themed books he's written. The Trump Taj Mahal's failure in 1991 was followed by Trump Plaza a year later, and really, how does a casino go bankrupt? Trump Hotel and Casino resorts suffered again in 2004, forcing him to rename the company Trump Entertainment, which itself filed for bankruptcy in 2014. Companies that have paid for his brand have also suffered: Coco Beach Golf and Country Club in Puerto Rico filed for creditor protection in 2015. It's almost as if anything with the name Trump on it turns to shit. Trump even co-authored a get-rich-quick paperback with fellow serial bankrupt, Robert Kiyosaki. Why anyone would take this chump's advice on business when there are real rags-to-riches stories to inspire us out there is one of life's great mysteries.

Despite the failures of his businesses however his books have sold well, proving one thing Trump is good at is lying about his success. Here then presents another opportunity to fleece individuals, the same type of customer who bought his books would be an easy target for Trump-branded seminars and courses on real estate. In fact why not just start your own entrepreneurial university? No prizes for guessing what it was called.

Trump University was founded in 2004 by The Donald and two associates with the aim of spreading the good word about real estate success to the masses. Actually with the aim of making naive customers pay extortionate amounts for shady advice that ultimately would cost them far more than they would ever make back. Calling it a 'university' was a stretch as it offered three to five-day courses and offered no accreditation or even grades. High-pressure sales tactics were used to get people to buy packages and after a while, the 'students' began to grumble.

In 2011, the state of New York opened an investigation. Not only did the state sue Trump in 2013, shutting down the university, but two class action settlements for fraud were brought by its attendees. Despite proudly insisting during his campaign that he would 'never settle,' President Trump eventually forked over $25 million. This is as good as a conviction for defrauding his customers. Mark Cuban, an actual self-made Billionaire commented on the talk show Real Time with Bill Maher in 2016, 'Has there been anyone who's come forward and said, Donald Trump has been a great mentor to me; I learned so much it helped me build my business? Has there been anyone who's come forward and said, I invested in Trump's business and I made so much money? No, all you see is, he took this, he stiffed me and he sucked.'

Those in search of success were not Trump's only victims. Altruists in need of spiritual succor and the needy who benefit from philanthropy were also easy prey for a charity called the Foundation for Ethical Giving. Just kidding: he called it the Donald J. Trump Foundation of course, and the name itself should have raised alarm bells from the start. It was just another opportunity to steal and was used as a front in several creative scams.

Begun in 1988, the foundation was initially created to spread the proceeds of his first book to worthy causes. For a number of years, Trump personally contributed but after 2008 seemed to tire of being a philanthropist and instead the organization relied entirely on solicited donations. By the time of the 2016 election, it was well known the charity was being used as a personal slush fund by the candidate and was already under investigation. Seeking to avoid election baggage, Trump tried to dissolve the foundation himself but was unable to do so as the courts were already involved. Crimes included failure to register in its home state of New York, self-dealing (we'll get to that) and that old favorite, a failure to disclose campaign finance contributions.

The second warning after the choice of name was the way the foundation was registered. As it was initially a private foundation set up to distribute donations only from the Trump family themselves, it did not have to submit to state auditors. Yet it was found in 2017 that Trump started soliciting outside donors between 1989 and 2004 without informing the proper authorities and creating a gap in oversight of almost two decades. What was his donors' money used for? Very little ever found its way to worthy causes.

The charity was also used as a front for bribery and palm-greasing. Grants were given to an 'art museum' that bought very little art, whose chairman was the head of the Building and Construction Trades Council, perhaps to solicit support when applying for building permits. Money was pledged to charities established for the families of first responders killed in the September 11 attacks, which never arrived. The foundation donated to a charity to restore the New Jersey governor's mansion while Trump's business was applying for a permit to build a golf course in that state; in 2013 when fraud allegations against Trump University were under review in Florida, the foundation donated to the re-election campaign of that state's attorney general Pam Bondi. Bondi's office dropped the investigation but the foundation was fined for donating to a political campaign, as it is illegal for charities to do so.

Trump's charity also played a role in his own campaign. Trump also used foundation money to make advantageous grants ahead of his presidential run, to The Billy Graham Evangelical Association, the Graham family's Samaritan's Purse and the conservative political lobby Citizens United at the time it was engaged in a lawsuit against the New York state Attorney General, which at the time was investigating Trump University. This was widely believed to be some kind of act of revenge. More directly, at a fundraiser in Iowa, money was collected that Trump's CFO Allen Weisselberg testified was directed toward his run for office.

The sleaze does not end there: in a blatant act of attempted vote-buying, the foundation donated to a 9/11 memorial Museum in New York on the eve of the presidential primary vote in the state in which he was running. During the campaign, the foundation also donated to Project Veritas, a shady organization that made propaganda videos smearing Trump's campaign rivals. Grants from the fund also paid for newspaper ads for the campaign, to curry support among conservative lobby groups, and Trump miscast donations made with foundation money as his own in order to talk himself up at rallies and interviews. You didn't think he'd actually use his own money did you? Not when there are willing donors to fleece.

When he pledged money for veterans causes and it was noted some weeks later he had not yet coughed up, Trump finally tapped the charity for that cash as well. This pledge can also be seen as campaigning as emotional support for members of the armed forces appeals to militaristic Republican voters.

Along the same lines, Trump has a long history of also diverting personal and business income to the charity in order to avoid paying taxes, to the tune of over two million dollars. Comedy Central, World Wrestling Entertainment, TV network NBC which hosted his show The Apprentice; People Magazine, a law office, and a cruise ship line are among the business that paid into Trump's 'charity' for celebrity appearances and endorsements by him or his family members. Charities that held events at his hotel also received donations, money which he personally recouped from the expense of their doing business with him – effectively laundering donor money back into his own pocket. These include the Dana Farber Cancer Institute, another cancer cause called The V-Foundation, the Palm Beach Police Foundation and others.

In some cases, Trump simply used the charity as a source of ready cash or to avoid paying his own bills. In at least one case, his lawyer Michael Cohen testified that Trump used $60,000 in charity funds to purchase a portrait of himself at auction which he later kept. This should have been a personal donation to the charity, not a withdrawal from it. Trump also paid for a luxury business trip to Paris out of foundation funds. In other cases, it was used to settle legal fees. In a property dispute with Palm Beach Florida, the county where Mar-a-Largo resort is located, Trump agreed to donate $100,000 to a local charity out of his own pocket. He used foundation money instead. The foundation spent another $158,000 to settle a dispute over prize money at a golf tournament held by one of Trump's clubs.

In all these cases we see Trump using the foundation and donor money to line his own pockets, pay his bills, further his business and political goals or as a front to hide income. Stealing is bad enough, but stealing from a charity should be a particular low for a US President. Yet to many of his supporters, who understand little of the business world beyond the movie Wall Street; who distrust the government and taxation and who think, like Trump, that getting ahead is a game of 'winners' and 'losers' and fortune favors the 'smart' ones who can find a shortcut, it seems a certain amount of graft can be tolerated. In 2019 the charity was disbanded by court order and the president was ordered to pay $2 million in fines and restitution.

The 45th president has even passed on the family business ethic to his children. Don Junior and Ivanka were under investigation in New York in 2012 for falsifying information to secure investors in their construction projects. Yet when the family's lawyer made a $25,000 donation to the District Attorney's re-election campaign, the case was quietly dropped. Add bribery to the list of financial crimes. As part of the charity court settlement, executive board members and familiar co-conspirators Don Jr. and Ivanka were ordered to take ethics counseling.

Trump also stole from his own supporters, and the country, while he was president. He promised a 1,600-mile border wall to keep Latin American migrants out, which he explicitly claimed on many occasions would be paid for by Mexico. He never explained how, of course, leaving it to his surrogates and mouthpieces to make up all manner of claims about macroeconomics and trade deficits to describe how in a roundabout way it would lead to Mexico funding the project. Yet two years into his presidency work hadn't even begun. By the end of the third year, what little progress had been made was being funded by the taxpayer or expropriated from the Pentagon budget – stealing from the troops this time.

Trump promised to repeal the Affordable Care Act, to be replaced with an unspecified 'better' healthcare program. Attempts to steal the people's health benefits have stalled in the courts. Like all Republicans, Trump promised massive tax cuts that would put more money in the back pockets of everyone; instead, the tax breaks mostly went to millionaires and corporations, robbing the national coffers of trillions in revenue. This would otherwise have been used to fund Medicare, the military, infrastructure and protection for the environment and national parks, yet most of these programs have seen cuts to make up for the loss in tax revenue, all taken instead from a nation of taxpayers who did not see significant cuts themselves.

And of course, what would the presidency be without the opportunity to make money from his office? While Trump famously pledged to take no salary from his role as president, he has instead committed the sort of 'high crimes and misdemeanors' that the so-called 'Emoluments Clause' was written into the Constitution to prevent: the use of a political position to accept gifts or titles from foreign dignitaries or to obtain favors and concessions at home. Trump has made it common practice to funnel foreign and government money into his various resorts and hotels. In fact, the group Citizens for Responsibility and Ethics in Washington counts over 2,000 potential conflicts of interest between Trump's presidency and businesses.

When foreign dignitaries and trade delegations chose to stay at Trump hotels to curry favor with the infamously greedy Trump, he directly profited from his position as the president. It is not even under the table. The visits from 57 foreign countries and hundreds of international business delegations violate the foreign gifts part of the Emoluments Clause, as much as the 59 foreign trademarks and patents issued to Trump businesses since he took office.

Trump supporters may argue he is just being 'smart' when he profits from his office, but it is dishonest in at least two ways. In the first instance, it steals business from less politically influential rivals and the so-called 'free market' that Republicans always laud is no longer free. In the second it opens the president to foreign influence, by attempting to please his business partners and clients. Given the way he has turned a blind eye to human rights abuses in places such as Saudi Arabia and Turkey, where he has interests and whose delegations stayed in his hotels, it seems to be working as planned.

Trump has hosted a number of conferences, state visits and campaign events at his own premises. When he invites foreign leaders to conferences at Mar-a-Largo or to Golf in New Jersey, he is not doing it for free. Though he pretends to have 'divested' himself of his business interests, in reality, he has only handed stewardship over to his eldest children, with whom he maintains a close working relationship. Trump does not even try to hide this graft. No sooner had he begin his presidency than he invited the Japanese Prime Minister to his Florida resort for a state visit. Since then he has hosted government officials from no fewer than fifty-seven foreign countries at his properties; taken at least a hundred golf trips at his own resorts, with his government entourage and paid for by the treasury, and hosted two dozen campaign events. Golf cart rental alone had cost the taxpayer over $550,000 by the middle of his first term.

This is not limited to his properties in the US. On a state visit to Ireland, Vice President Pence made an unnecessary detour to Doonbeg, one of Trump's Irish golf clubs; his motorcade reportedly driving hours out of its way to do so. Trump himself insisted on flying hundreds of miles out of the way to visit the same hotel ahead of D-Day celebrations in France. Either it was mixing his private business with a state visit in order to save time – something as a divested individual he should not be doing – or a calculated stop to funnel government money into his own resort. Along similar lines, military crews have made over 200 unscheduled stopovers at his Turnberry golf club in Scotland while their aircraft refueled at a nearby airport that never saw as much use before his presidency. This resort alone had gained an estimated $200,000 in revenue from the visits by the time the scam was exposed.

At home again, accommodation for security details and other basics are funneled to his businesses. Those Secret Service agents need rooms, food and showers; cabinet members and White House functionaries at least need the internet; the foreign dignitaries and Republican Party officials no doubt need hookers and blow. In an early 2020 report, the Washington Post revealed the Secret Service had spent over half a million in taxpayer money at Trump properties – in some case for $650-a-night rooms – all money going into the president's bottom line. In many cases the price of the rooms were inflated when the customer was the US government paying for his security detail.

Campaign events and fundraisers are held at Trump hotels and resorts using donor money and even Republican National Committee funds. This amounts to a domestic political organization donating to his businesses even as he benefits from its political support – just the sort of quid pro quo proscribed in the Emoluments Clause. It doesn't end there: over a hundred members of Congress and 47 state officials, including 20 governors have visited and spent money at Trump properties, as well as 64 political groups for campaign events. Trump White House staff have plugged his resorts at least sixty times in TV interviews, press conferences, speeches and on social media, violating the Hatch Act, a piece of legislation that also prohibits politicians and public officials from self-dealing. Foreign governments have held two dozen events at Trump resorts and that is in addition to the various visits and stays by dignitaries and delegates. All told Trump's trips to and hosting at his own properties have netted the president's businesses millions of dollars, making his 'foregone' salary a pittance by comparison.

Those times when Trump rallies and fundraisers were not held at his own properties to his own profit, and the citizens of the United States have been in a position to bill Trump for his events, he has been less than forthcoming in paying the actual hosts back. The businessman who stiffed his contractors has become the president who dodges his bills. This should come as no surprise. In 2019, Business Insider posted a list of some of the cities across at least five states seeking reimbursement for police overtime and enhanced security at Trump events that were in some cases three years outstanding. El Paso, Albuquerque, Minneapolis, Tucson and Spokane all sought between $65,000 and $569,000. Albuquerque mayor Tim Keller stated, 'We are asking the Trump campaign to pay our taxpayers back for the costs from his campaign stop.' There is no ambiguity here.

So far all this financial dishonesty hasn't cost Trump an ounce of Evangelical support despite the Bible proclaiming in the Book of Romans, one should 'Pay to all what is owed to them: taxes to whom taxes are owed, revenue to whom revenue is owed.'

Some suggest that Trump had never expected to win the presidency and that his intention all along had been merely to fleece donors, shore up his name, funnel money to his properties where events were hosted and garner support for a planned right-wing cable network predictably named Trump TV. If Trump's only plan was to make money, he did not even wait a single day after taking office to continue fleecing the public. Campaign money and funds raised from donors for his inauguration were by law supposed to be used for the stated public purposes. However, in early 2020 after a years-long investigation, the Washington D.C. district attorney charged that $300,000 in donor cash was used to fund a private inauguration party for the family, but also that up to $1 million in donor money was spent putting up inauguration staff and officials at Trump's luxury hotel in the capital. A further $3.6 million was spent renting the hotel's convention venue. Not only did the Trump clan have the audacity to use his own hotel, thumbing his nose at the Emoluments Clause on day one of his presidency, but the DC attorney's investigation began when it received evidence that the Trump property had indulged in price gouging – inflating rates and fees just for that event. Adding credence to the notion his entire presidential run was just a scheme to enrich himself and his family, Trump himself boasted during one campaign speech,

'It's very possible that I could be the first presidential candidate to run and make money on it.'

Stealing money is one thing, stealing an election is a bigger fish entirely. The main mechanism for this is undermining the right to vote. The History of Republican voter suppression only goes back some 40 or 50 years. Before that, was southern Democrats who upheld segregation and the notorious Jim Crow laws that denied African Americans their basic rights. But when the Democratic Party embraced racial inclusiveness and civil rights, segregationist Democrats in Southern states defected to the Republican party. Thereafter the 'Party of Lincoln,' who ironically fought to free the slaves, developed the Southern Strategy, an electoral campaign plan to pander to these racist states and exclude as many black people from the democratic process as it could. Republican election strategists have since been caught on tape admitting as much, and as recently as 2019, emails and files held by state and national campaign operatives and even White House officials have were leaked to the press supporting this aim.

Most of this battle is fought in state legislatures and federal courts. Conservative judges and officials have embarked on a decades-long campaign not just to discourage voting by people of color, who since the Civil Rights era have overwhelmingly supported the Democrats, but to effectively prohibit it. One of the tricks is gerrymandering; a tactic used by both sides wherein the party in power in a state redraws districts to effectively hold onto a political seat. The technique breaks up opposing voting blocks and redistributes the diluted numbers across several districts by cutting lines through ethnic or sectarian communities that vote for one party while keeping districts that vote for the party in power largely together. This is called 'cracking' a district, an ironic term given who mostly does it and to whom.

The other gerrymandering method involved is 'packing' which simply shovels all opposition voters into districts that they're already likely to hold on to (while cracking other districts to give one's own party more to room play with) so their votes effectively become wasted. This ensures the opposition is a permanent minority, even where they may have superior numbers. The GOP has been more effective at this, especially in southern states. Gerrymandering has even spread to northern rural states and districts where the GOP holds power: in Wisconsin Republicans only won 48% of the vote but in doing so took 61% of the districts. This effectively dilutes people's votes.

A more sinister technique is manipulating electoral rolls. In many states, laws have been drafted that make it easier to strike registered voters off the rolls and harder for those removed to get back on. Purging rolls is often necessary as people die, go to prison and lose the right to vote (at least for a while) or simply move away. However, this is often done simply on the basis of name or voting history and with no investigation into whether an individual should be struck off or not. Research by organizations such as the Southern Poverty Law Center shows that in Republican-held states, names common to African Americans and Hispanics such as Washington or Hernandez, are more often removed than 'white' names. Sometimes hundreds of people who share the name with a single felon or deceased individual are removed, just for the hell of it. It takes the stroke of a pen to remove a name, but litigation to get re-enrolled is costly and time-consuming, getting tied up in the courts for months or years, which effectively results in potential voters missing elections.

This happened in the 2018 gubernatorial election in Georgia, where the Republicans narrowly won, but their victory was stained by the near 60,000 reinstatement applications that were stalled in the lead-up. The state's white Republican attorney general, who ran for governor and won, refused to process these applications before the election. In Wisconsin in early 2020, the appeals court blocked an attempt to fast-track the purging of up to 200,000 minority voters ahead of that year's presidential election. The Republicans are stealing votes in other words.

In addition to cutting voters off, GOP-led districts have raised the bar for voting. Since the early 2000s, Republicans have cited the almost non-existent crime of voter fraud as their main cause. This allegedly involves people such as non-citizens or felons illegally casting ballots under another name, or casting more than one. It is nonsense of course: researchers at Loyola University found in almost two decades of state, federal and presidential elections, only 31 credible cases in over a billion votes cast. Nevertheless, Republicans have rammed through laws demanding voters have drivers licenses, certain proof of address and other forms of identification. Those who never needed to prove who they were before are suddenly challenged when enrolling or when turning up to vote. If they cannot provide the relevant I.D. on the spot they are turned away.

This disproportionately affects people on the lower socio-economic scale, again people of color and those who tend to vote Democrat, as it can be costly and time-consuming to obtain the relevant I.D. Those who don't drive need to get a driver's license; those who don't travel abroad need a passport; those who don't read much or don't go to the library need a library card; those with no fixed address or who cannot produce a certificate proving they live are denied enrolment. One North Carolina federal court found that the methods targeted African Americans with 'almost surgical precision.'

Other minorities are also targeted: in some cases whole communities of Native Americans living on reservations and using P.O. Box addresses have been stricken off because their states suddenly required a street address. In South Dakota, the GOP led state legislature has deemed that tribal I.D. cards will no longer be accepted for voter registration. Since when did

Native Americans need to prove they were 'natural-born' Americans? They got here first. Now the Republicans are stealing the right to vote.

Finally by closing polling stations in certain districts, moving them far away, creating long queues and misinforming voters, Republicans make it physically harder to vote. On election dates, both local and national, voters have waited until polls closed without having the chance to cast their ballots. In other instances Republican campaign officials or interest groups have sent mailouts to districts with the wrong date, time or location, creating confusion and delays or missed opportunities. Again this has been done where the likelihood of opposition votes is strong: now a white minority in a multi-ethnic country, Republicans benefit when fewer people vote not more. Hundreds of districts have been shaken up in this way since the shock win of a black man in the presidential election in 2008, something the GOP is determined to avoid a repeat of. In January 2020, the 9th Circuit Court of Appeals denied efforts of the Republican-led Arizona state legislature to funnel minority voters into specific polling stations, finding that it was targeted at Black, Hispanic and Native Americans and designed to stop them using the convenience of 'Out of Precinct' voting mechanisms; stealing the chance to vote.

Lately, not content just to close the polling stations, or trick people into not turning up, intimidation at the polls has become more common. From police and state officials demanding I.D. to bearded and armed militias hanging around in camouflage 'challenging' people of color to prove who they are, voting has begun to take on the air of danger one would expect in turbulent African dictatorships.

These methods all make it much easier for Republicans to win an election. Nationally, the Republicans hold a slim majority of seats in the Senate, but represent only a third of the electorate, as many as ten million fewer voters than the Senate's Democratic minority. Efforts were stepped up ahead of the 2020 elections. Perhaps hastened by their loss of the House of Representatives in the 2018 mid-terms, GOP strategists deployed a nationwide strategy of moving and closing polling stations, striking names of rolls, repealing the recently-won right of felons to vote in Florida and finding ways to subvert the provisions of the Voting Rights Act, such as moving polling stations away from college campuses, where younger, more liberal voters reside. According to the American Civil Liberties Union, the five states with the highest voter turnout in 2018 all introduced the toughest voting laws and regulations after 2018; after record turnout in 2008, 30 states introduced legislation that would make it harder for people to vote. Nationwide at least 17 million voters were purged from rolls between 2016 and 2018. After winning the presidency and the Senate, the Republicans were trying to close the door behind them, ensuring they never got voted out again by stealing people's ability to vote.

These measures have been hastened by a conservative-led Supreme Court ruling that allowed Republicans to argue that parts of the landmark Voting Rights Act were no longer needed because, apparently, discrimination has ended. You could say it has simply evolved. At the same time, the Republicans pushed through 'Citizens United' legislation that identifies corporations as 'groups' of voters and lets them make almost unlimited campaign donations. So even as they silence the voice of individuals, they open the door to moneyed interests, just like the plantation owners of yesteryear. And the pieces have been in place for a long time: one of the founders of the modern conservative movement, Paul Weyrich said in a 1980 speech to Republicans, 'I don't want everybody to vote...our leverage in the elections quite candidly goes up as the voting populace goes down.'

This has helped Republicans immensely. They consistently hold more state legislatures than the democrats, have had the opportunity to appoint more conservative justices to the supreme court to uphold some of their attacks on voting rights and the last Republican-led Congress represented over ten million voters fewer than the minority Democrats. It matters in presidential elections as well: in the last quarter century Republicans have won three out of six presidential races in the Electoral College but have only taken the popular vote once. The country consistently votes blue.

Though Donald Trump benefitted from Republican-led voter suppression in the 2016 and 2020 elections, it was not enough to win the second time. He lost the popular vote in the former by several million to Hillary Clinton, but scratched out a win in a few key counties that allowed him to take the majority of the states. In the latter, the gap between Trump and Joe Biden was nearer to ten million and insurmountable: Biden won in a landslide. At this point Trump and his GOP enablers moved on to Plan B. If preventing people from voting is not enough, let's just steal their votes after the fact. Indeed let's just steal the entire election.

Trump showed his hand in 2016 when he started claiming early and loudly the only way he could lose the election is if it was rigged. This was a stunning claim for a candidate to make and was more or less an admission he'd be a sore loser. Yet his followers bought in and he used the excuse even after the election to explain the three million more votes gained by his opponent Hillary Clinton. In 2020 he continued the 'rigged' claim, despite being the incumbent. This time, he *did* lose and now had the opportunity put the collective delusion of a rigged election to the test.

Part of the process was to keep lying. This was the important promotional aspect, with Trump and his surrogates in the media complaining loud and often that the election was stolen, and will be covered in the next chapter about bearing false witness. Yet the how-to of stealing an election consisted of not just talk, but a number of specific and demonstrably criminal actions – all of which Trump the Department of Justice indicted Mr. Trump for after he reluctantly left office.

The first was Obstruction of an Official Proceeding: After the election of November 2020 in which Trump lost, there was a two-month interim before the next administration took over on January 20. Pivotal to this and every election is the day about two weeks before that when Congress certifies the results of the electoral college and the sitting Vice President presides. Trump sought for weeks to lobby his own Vice President Mike pence to give him the result he wanted, not the results of the ballot. Trump wanted Pence to simply ignore the will of the electorate and let him stay on as president.

When Pence ignored the lobbying Trump took to the airwaves to make public calls for him to 'do the right thing' and finally on the afternoon of January 6th, he held a rally outside the Capitol while the certification was in process and famously fired up an angry mob to sack the place, chanting 'Hang Mike Pence!' Rioters and police were injured and killed, congressmen and the vice president were forced to flee the premises and after the noise died down they returned and Pence did the right thing: he certified the election results. Given that for a few hours – and with resulting loss of life, injury to persons and damage to property – the proceeding was indeed interrupted at Trump's behest, he was charged with this crime. It carries a maximum penalty of twenty years.

The next was Conspiracy to Obstruct an Official Proceeding: not merely the action of the former, but the intent to do so and attempts to threaten, coerce and cajole others into doing his bidding. This involved a multi-pronged effort that culminated in the Jan 6 attempted overthrow of the electoral process. He began by pressuring state lawmakers not to accept the results in their districts, where those results did not favor Donald Trump. He also pressured the department of Justice and Attorney General Bill Barr to open a bogus investigation into the allegedly 'stolen' election. Knowing the law better than Trump, Mr. Barr demurred. Many co-conspirators did play along however and later found themselves in court on criminal charges for conspiring to defraud the country, tampering with the election process and impersonating election officials.

All this was underpinned by a month's long publicity campaign. For this cheap demagoguery, Trump was charged with Conspiracy to Defraud the United States. Trump simultaneously sought to nominate an alternate slate of state electors – all party loyalists – who would undermine their state's already appointed electors whose duty was to turn up on January 6th and submit state results to congress and the Vice President. This was discovered and failed and a paper trail a mile long was left in emails and other documents. Next under this charge, Trump was accused of soliciting the mob he gathered on the day, when he gave his speech that day in front of Congress.

In so doing, Team Trump sought to exploit the riot *that he himself caused* by demanding that the proceedings be halted and reconvened another day, thus obstructing the proceeding. This charge carries a maximum of five years. In the event Trump failed, but his intention was to have a 'recount' as it were, with Mike Pence delivering the result Trump wanted this time – assuming he hadn't yet been hanged.

The final charge is based on an old post Civil War statute written to prevent the Ku Klux Klan intimidating African American voters: Conspiracy to prevent others carrying out their constitutional right. In soliciting fake state electors, the attorney general and finally an angry mob to attempt to overturn both the popular vote and the results in the electoral college, Trump was also attempting to deny the will of the voters themselves. This one carries a maximum penalty often years.

Trump's actions were not limited to Washington DC on January 6th. He also used surrogates or directly appealed to election officials in other states to overturn the narrow margins of loss that he suffered there. Late on the night of the election, exit polls showed Joe Biden ahead in many key battleground states. Trump publicly called for the counting to stop before all votes were tabulated. As the count was still underway in Georgia, Trump called its Secretary of State and in a famously taped telephone call, asked him to 'find 11,780 votes, one more than we need.' Trump has been indicted under several felony conspiracy charges in Georgia for this. In Arizona, Trump surrogates including Rudy Giuliani also attempted to tamper with local numbers, including conspiring with surrogates to interfere with voting machines and calling election officials to pressure them. These officials, many of them Republicans, put duty before party and refused to take his calls. The schemes in both states involved intimidating election officials and even plans to tamper with voting machines. All have since been indicted locally, generating famous mug shots of Giuliani and Trump.

To top it off, when Mr. Trump finally did leave the White House, he took with him hundreds of documents from his time as President, many of which were highly classified. He kept these papers in dozens of boxes at his Florida resort residence, some unsecured in a disused bathroom and others in a laundry cupboard. When the government lawyers asked Trump to return the papers he refused and the FBI had to raid the place to recover them. He was subsequently indicted by the Department of Justice again, this time for the theft of government property.

Moreover, since the New York attorneys felt obliged to wait until Trump left office, it wasn't until 2023 that they built their case and brought charges for his attempts to defraud the people in the 2016 election, by hiding hush money payments to the adult film actress he'd slept with. This meant that by 2024, the number of charges against Trump in New York, Georgia and Washington DC numbered a whopping 88 separate counts. This was in addition to those against his co-conspirators in Michigan,

Pennsylvania and Arizona for attempting to sway the 2020 election in Trump's favor by pressuring election officials or conspiring to name fake electors.

After losing the election, Trump continued to grift. His campaign website immediately set about soliciting donors via email with promises to put their money into a fund to challenge the 2020 results. The Guardian reports that no such fund was set up and Trump gathered roughly $250 million by the end of the year. Trump kept making money off his election loss well into the next year. Trump's websites and those of the Political Action Committees that raised money for him, found ways to fleece donors of more than they had signed up to pay. They aggressively emailed Republican Voters, previous donors and anyone on known lists of supporters with exhortations to 'Stop the steal,' repeating Trump's stolen election slogan, cajoling them with promises of becoming gold-member style donors and elites among the MAGA faithful, and even coercing them with threats of earning the former president's displeasure.

Even 'small donations' of a few hundred dollars can be big money to the many retirees rural poor and blue collar stiffs who supported the president. Yet when signing on for a single donation many online donors may have missed the small checkbox that told them the donation would automatically recur monthly or weekly if they didn't manually uncheck it. Many Trump supporters reported losing several thousand dollars before they noticed the money was still going out and demanding a refund.

Some did not even know they were donating to Trump. In several cases, PACs disguised the true aim of the donation – to raise money for Trump's alleged post 2020 legal challenges against the election results – as run-of-the-mill donations to the local Republican party branch and its various needs. Donors believed their payments to sites such as Republican fundraising platform WinRed would be used by the party in local elections for down-ballot candidates: these were not only recurring but diverted mostly to the Trump campaign (either for 2024 or against 2020, take your pick at this point). In 2021, the courts forced the Trump campaign to pay back $122 million in illicitly seized donor contributions.

The Trump campaign's use of the money was murkier still. While Trump also openly solicited donations to help him fight his legal battles, the fine print on some of Trump's general campaign donation pages mentioned that by signing on, the donors consented to the majority of the money instead being diverted to the Trump Organization – his business empire. From here, the money was then spent on Trump's various legal battles, including those for tax fraud related to his real estate properties and personal defamation suits by women who had accused him of sexual assault. In all by 2023 Trump's legal bills amounted to over fifty million dollars of mostly other people's money in, not to mention the $84 million he had to pay in a defamation settlement to one female accuser early the following year. Many die-hard Trump supporters might be happy to find out later their election campaign donations were misappropriated in this way. The 'billionaire' grafter sure wasn't paying for it himself.

With a complicit GOP, the 45th President of the United States, a lifelong crook and fraudster, attempted to pull off the biggest score of even his shady and litigious career. He was now participating in the grand theft of American democracy itself by eroding the rights of Americans to vote, if they might vote against him and seeking to overturn the vote after the fact when it didn't go his way. He did this with lies, intimidation, conspiracies and failing that, violence, when he sent a mob to disrupt the election certification and intimidate lawmakers and the vice president. In effect, this was an attempted coup to steal democracy itself. When that failed, he kept making excuses to take even more money from hardworking Americans whom he had fooled into following him. Most of his supporters are okay with this because apparently, God chose Trump to do great things despite his personal flaws. Among those and perhaps the most famous, is his utter inability to tell the truth.

9. THOU SHALT NOT BEAR FALSE WITNESS

'He's spent millions of dollars in legal fees trying to get away from this issue…and I'm starting to wonder myself whether or not he was even born in this country.'

- Exaggerations, 4:34

On 11 June 2024, Donald J. Trump, the erstwhile 45th President of the United States, held a Zoom meeting with his probation officer. He had just been convicted on 34 counts of fraud related to the 2016 election. Accompanied by his lawyer, Trump's interview lasted less than thirty minutes and was standard procedure in the state of New York before attending his sentencing date. In new York defendants – at least white collar ones - are given the choice of an in-person or video interview. Presumably exhausted by the repeated court dates in which he was often seen nodding off, Trump chose the latter. Just let that sink in. A former President of the Unites States convicted of a felony and prior to sentencing obliged to meet his probation officer.

All politicians are liars. This is not only the common refrain we hear from Trump supporters – even those on the religious Right who are supposed to disapprove of lying no matter who does it – but it is also common sense. A typical politician may exaggerate his achievements or the benefits of a proposal. He may downplay his failures or mischaracterize a competitor's words or intentions. He might take credit for achievements that are only partly his own; he may deny an extra-marital affair or a historical driving offense out of both embarrassment and political expediency. The lying of a normal politician is a means to an end, a way to gain and hold votes, often with his main policy goals and what he perceives as the greater good in mind.

Donald Trump, however, is a breed apart. His lies, mistruths, half-truths and 'alternative facts' transcend mere politics. He is a habitual and instinctive liar; a man who cannot help lying. He seems to have a poor grasp of the truth even when it might benefit him. His falsehoods are far removed from the everyday lies you and I might tell, or the career-motivated misrepresentations that are the stock in trade any normal politician.

On its Wikipedia page, pathological lying is defined as 'falsification entirely disproportionate to any discernible end in view; it may be extensive and very complicated, and may manifest over a period of years or even a lifetime.' This describes Trump in a nutshell. He lies to aggrandize himself; he lies to slander his political opponents, and anyone he considers an enemy, frenemy or business rival; he lies to downplay his shady associations or to cover his mistakes and his lack of knowledge and experience; he lies because he doesn't care what the truth is or who finds out; he lies because it's Tuesday and he just feels like it.

By the end of his third year in office, fact-checkers had tracked a total of over 16,000 public lies told by the president on Twitter, in TV interviews, public addresses, rally speeches, and press conferences. This adds up to fifteen lies a day on average, told to the whole world watching. In one 2020 speech alone to a group of New York business leaders, CNN reported Trump made 29 false claims in seventy minutes – one every two minutes. According to the news service, 'His address to the Economic Club of New York was littered with inaccurate economic statistics, baseless claims about environmental policy, and one of his signature fictional tales about people crying in gratitude at one of his events.' A classic mix of lying about the numbers (the economy), mischaracterizing an opponent (in this case science) and pointless self-praise (the teary-eyed fan). In the same speech, the president also claimed his polls were higher than ever, even while actual media polls showed he was plumbing historic lows – something easily and instantly disproven by anyone in the room with a smart phone.

Tracking the falsehoods in Trump's speeches and tweets has become something of a media fact-checker's spectator sport, with similar minutes-to-lies ratios and daily tallies. By the end of his term he had been documented lying in public a whopping 30,573 times. Some might say he was just warming up.

Perhaps not incidentally, pathological lying is high on the checklist mental health experts use to identify psychopaths. It has already been described how Trump's alter ego 'spokesmen' called into Forbes to inflate his wealth. This is a typically self-serving lie and a brazen one if he had planned to use the Forbes listing he obtained to secure loans. He probably did it at first just because he wanted to be in the club. Likewise, his surrogate boasts about womanizing and being approached by pop stars such as Madonna appear to be ego-driven as well. As discussed, many of his financial crimes and frauds began with lies: lies to the IRS, local authorities; assessors, insurers, investors and customers. These were no doubt told for expediency in his business dealings and are the lies of a common con-artist; a used car salesman who deliberately winds back the odometer.

Good lies have a grain of truth. This doesn't mean you won't get caught, but allows plausible deniability. When a politician touts the projected economic value of a project or the number of jobs a policy may create, the figures are usually not entirely unreasonable, even if they later fail to deliver. They may disingenuously include or exclude other contributing factors to suit the narrative, but they are grounded in at least some degree of fact. Not so with Trump. When he lies, he lies big and he lies often – like the bodybuilder's T-shirt says, 'go heavy or go home.' Trump lies casually and nonchalantly about his success, inflating his net worth by orders of magnitude, or boasting about his wealth and his acquisitions. 'If you don't tell people about your success, they probably won't know about it.' If he really were as rich and successful as he claims to be, everybody probably would already know. It is just another insight perhaps into the insecure child inside of Donald Trump, that despite his actual wealth, he still needs to exaggerate.

On the campaign trail, Trump lied often enough about himself but was also obliged to put some policy out there to get votes. Again, most politicians will embellish their plans to create jobs, grow the economy, develop infrastructure or improve national security, but Trump really had no plans outside of hating on foreigners in general, Muslims and Mexicans in particular. With no vision for the country and no actual policies to underpin his ephemeral platform of making America 'great' again, he was free to make up anything he liked on the spot.

What followed during the campaign was an increasingly detached series of rallies where Trump hugged the flag, boasted about his wealth, his daughter's beauty and even in one debate, the size of his dick, all while he railed against the usual bugbears: Mexicans, Socialists, China, the Clintons and Whoopi Goldberg. These were all great crowd-pleasers but hardly constitute policy. Still, he sprinkled enough hyperbolic substance to satisfy the few supporters who cared about something other than being armed, white and empowered.

He promised more jobs, millions more, without saying where they'd come from. In the end his mishandling of the Covid-19 pandemic resulted in a net loss of tens of millions of jobs. When he had a specific industry in mind it was usually obsolete ones such as coal (giving way to green energy such as wind power and unlikely to make a comeback) and steel (undercut permanently by foreign players such as China) and other typically blue-collar jobs that white 'rust belt' voters were losing. Both continued to decline well into his presidency to be replaced by green energy such as wind turbines, which Trump claims 'cause cancer.' And coal doesn't?

He promised tax cuts to everyone because it plays well but had no numbers on how much each household would save, or what it might cost them in social services and infrastructure. Instead the most wealthy got large permanent tax cuts and the middle class got small temporary ones. He promised to repeal the Affordable Care Act, derided as Obamacare by many of his supporters who weren't even aware they benefitted from it and promised to replace it with 'something better.' To the end of his term he never elaborated what that better is and no effort has been made to formulate a new health program, despite consistently targeting cuts to existing ones.

Trump also lied maliciously, testing audience reactions for the perfect lightning rods: In marketing, the term A/B testing or 'bucket testing' refers to giving a target audience two choices to see which they like/dislike more. In a Trump speech that meant railing against one supposed villain or another, noting which ones elicited the loudest jeers and then revisiting that target again and again. China remains a favorite because it is foreign, ethnically and culturally different, ostensibly communist and a genuine economic competitor. While it is true some trade imbalance exists and that Chinese firms are less than kosher about copyright, it is hard to say China is stealing jobs when it simply produces many goods more cheaply and efficiently than American industry can. Mexico was another easy target. Trump claimed famously in his campaign announcement speech that migrants coming across the border were narcotics traffickers and sex offenders, and that Mexico was not 'sending their best people' and they were rapists and drug smugglers. In the real world, undocumented immigrants and overstayers commit crime at a far lower rate than native-born Americans; moreover, those fleeing corruption, poverty and violence were hardly being 'sent,' and most were from other Latin American states. Nevertheless, this also played well with fearful, xenophobic supporters.

In a similar vein Trump promised to ban all Muslims from entering the country, 'Until we figure out what the hell is going on,' another off-the-cuff rant that appealed to his base, and that his policy team later narrowed to citizens of a few hostile or conflict-plagued countries in order to make it look like he'd actually thought it through. The ban however was stalled in various federal courts as discrimination based on religion was deemed unconstitutional. As always, Trump was just telling people what he thought they wanted to hear at the time and had no plans to follow up. He has no vision of his own for the country, so he simply co-opted the emotions that pushed peoples' buttons.

Some of Trump's exaggerations hit closer to home. Guns and abortion are favorites of the Christian Right and he wasted no time in claiming that Democrats want to take everyone's firearms or repeating internet rumors that federally funded family planning clinics were sponsoring forced abortions. He went as far in the presidential debates, on live TV and in front of his opponent Hillary Rodham Clinton, to paint a grim picture of late-term fetuses 'ripped' from their mothers' wombs, causing shock and horror on both sides of the debate: on the one hand, the gory rendition elicited the desired reaction from disgusted pro-lifers; on the other, this lurid mischaracterization of the procedure incensed the liberal opposition.

Once in office, rather than doing any actual work, the pathological lying accelerated. As the Trump administration lurched from one legal or PR scandal to another, the solution was always to lie big on-screen and leave someone else to clean up the mess. When the tax cuts turned out to benefit only the wealthy, Trump took credit for the steady growth in jobs and a climbing Dow Jones index that started under his predecessor Obama. This handily deflected from the fact most middle and low-income families would not see a significant cut in taxes and that wages were still stagnant while millions were living paycheck to paycheck. When it all crashed during the Covid pandemic, it was someone else's fault of course.

Trump inflates all manner of figures at random: He claimed once his daughter Ivanka's businesses had created a whopping 14 million jobs over a two year period when the entire economy had only added 6 million. Nobody on his side cared in the least. When he was criticized for his support of the Saudi Regime under Prince Mohammed Bin Salman, often chided for its poor human rights record including the murder of a dissident journalist at its Turkish embassy, his defense was the profitable sale of weapons and military equipment to the kingdom worth $100 billion dollars. The Saudis were negotiating an air-defense upgrade at that point but Pentagon estimates placed it at only around $14 billion, or about an eighth of Trump's figure. Undeterred, Trump added the deal would create half a million jobs, which he then later randomly inflated to a million. The mere tens of thousands of jobs actually involved were already people employed in the industry. Defense contractors cannot just grab anyone off the street and put them to work in a missile factory.

The economy seems to be an easy topic to lie about, as it is not really a strong suit among Trump's rural followers. When the Bureau of Labor Statistics reported 128,000 jobs were added in October 2019, Trump tweeted 303,000; in the 2016 campaign he claimed the trade deficit was 'nearly $800 billion' when the actual figure was only $531 billion; the 2017 deficit with China sat at $335 billion when Trump asserted 'A lot of people think it's $506 billion.' When Trump begins with his trademark openers, 'I'm hearing' and 'a lot of people are saying,' it's usually a sign he's making shit up again and hasn't even bothered to research it.

A sore winner, Trump couldn't handle the notion that he had lost the popular vote by almost three million in 2016 and immediately claimed that was the number of illegal immigrants voting for his opponent, then inflated the figure to 'as many as 5 million' in the next breath. He claimed one million illegal votes were cast in California alone, though his own failed electoral fraud commission found nothing of the sort; he created 58,000 illegal votes in Texas out of thin air. Nationwide cases of in-person voter fraud, be it noncitizens casting ballots, people voting twice or under the wrong name or voting when ineligible, amounted to only a handful in any given state: usually in the single digits, and half of the cases having voted for Trump. High profile cases of voters illegally registered in two states included Trump's future Treasury secretary Steven Mnuchin, campaign adviser Steve Bannon and his second daughter Tiffany Trump. Of course his own supporters are legion, but it will never be enough for the perpetually greedy and insecure Donald: in February of 2020 he proudly boasted of 'forty to fifty thousand' attendees at his New Hampshire primary rally; while there was some overflow of a few hundred into the car park, the venue's capacity was less than 12,000,

Conversely, Trump casually deflates figures when it comes to the cost of his pipe dreams, just as he did when trying to get a tax break on his properties. When asked how much the wall would cost he simply grabbed a number, around $12 billion, which sounded pretty cheap. Experts and government departments expected it would be anywhere between $20 and $45 billion over a decade or more, but when Trump was challenged on the numbers, he simply claimed 'Mexico's gonna pay for it,' another of his election rally promises that always elicits a cheer but has no basis in fact. In the absence of any substance or detail, it is left to some of his supporters and surrogates to make up fuzzy math, voodoo economics and wild stories about the merits of projected trade surpluses to somehow justify the claims; most just don't even blink and take it as it is.

When Trump is in trouble or a scandal is brewing his tactic is similarly transparent: deny all knowledge, much like a three-year-old who just broke a vase. Confronted with women who have accused him of sexual assault, his initial stance is that he has never met them. When photos have emerged of them meeting at events or lining up for publicity shots, he may then resort to claiming the woman was not attractive enough to bother with. During the defamation trial of 2023 and 2024 brought by journalist E. Jean Carroll, Trump was shown photos of himself and his alleged victim Carroll from the nineties and mistakenly identified Carroll as his wife at the time. A court eventually found that Carroll had not been lying when she alleged Trump assaulted her and therefore he had defamed her for claiming so and awarded her $83 million of his donor's money.

As for his affairs, again Trump claimed to have never met the women, even after documents show money changed hands or pictures emerge of them smiling for the cameras at one of his events. The same goes for shady lawyers and other business associates. One week he can be heard extolling a friend or acquaintance's virtues, the next 'I hardly knew the guy,' as was the case with sex-offender Jeffrey Epstein, with whom Trump had been photographed and filmed multiple times; or his personal lawyer of many years Michael Cohen, jailed for conspiring to conceal hush-money payments to Trump's mistresses. One of the more recent accusers is Lev Parnas, a Ukrainian witness embroiled in the president's impeachment over withholding aid to that country in return for political favors, who has been photographed dozens of times not just in the company of Trump, but with members of his legal team such as Pam Bondi and new personal lawyer Rudy Giuliani. When confronted about his association with Parnas, Trump responded, 'I don't know who this man is.' Parnas released pictures of them shaking hands and posing, the following day, and a few days later, a tape of Trump ordering him and others in the room to get the US ambassador to Ukraine fired.

Trump is not content to merely tell his own lies. He is an active disseminator of internet rumors and conspiracy theories, especially on Twitter. He has pushed stories that suit his own narratives, such as the notion it was Ukraine via Crowdstrike that interfered in the 2016 election on behalf of Clinton. This is perhaps understandable for a politician seeking greater legitimacy, but the story has been debunked many times by leaks, investigative journalism and congressional committees. Seventeen intelligence agencies including the FBI, CIA and NSA have all confirmed it was Russia's cyber warfare division that interfered and it most likely did so to help Trump.

Though the president has the most authoritative sources available on earth in media, intelligence agencies, think tanks, policy centers; entire branches and departments of government dealing with the economy, foreign affairs, the environment, healthcare, and legal matters, Trump seemed content getting a lot of his stock claims from right-wing internet forums and blogs such as 4chan and Stormfront. These run the gamut of internet conspiracies: global warming is a hoax, vaccines cause autism, Muslims want to enforce Sharia law in the US, Obama paid a ransom to Iran in return for hostages; a deceased supreme court justice may have been assassinated; Republican senator Ted Cruz's father may have been involved in the Kennedy assassination and his own building was wiretapped during the 2016 election. Hurricane death tolls are overestimated, wind turbines cause cancer, Jeffrey Epstein did not commit suicide in his cell but was murdered. All of these are either unfounded or have been disproved and all of them have been repeated many times by Trump either in tweets, TV interviews or at speeches, campaign rallies and election debates.

When claiming Ukraine was hiding a secret computer server containing stolen emails (or something) Trump dodged the hard evidence: 'Well that's what the word is,' he told interviewers on FOX News. Could it be that when Trump 'hears' things it's just him, doom scrolling and retweeting any garbage he finds useful, expedient or unflattering to his opponents? The Congressional Budget Office, Pentagon, Treasury Department, Homeland Security, CIA, Weather Service and EPA routinely contradict the president's claims, yet he goes on 'hearing' things. Perhaps it's that burning bush at it again. Perhaps like Abraham, God speaks to him directly.

These excuses are enough because Trump doesn't care if he gets caught lying. He has no sense of shame and little use for the truth. As a spoiled rich boy, surrounded by yes-men in both his business and political careers, he has likely rarely been challenged on his positions in private. For many of his claims – jobs figures, tax cut benefits, the cost of projects and programs, the benefits and drawbacks of trade deals and the number of people who voted for him or didn't – the fact-checkers can easily crunch the numbers, pull out a chart or cite a study and disprove him the following day. By then it is too late. Trump supporters don't care because outsiders or the 'Deep State' are out to get; Trump doesn't notice because his inner circle assures him he's right. Despite eyewitness evidence if Trump says it, it is real. His true believers hear what they want to and disseminate it widely. Any correction that comes after can be dismissed as 'fake news.' As White House spokesperson Kellyanne Conway once famously responded, when confronted on CNN with uncomfortable statistics about Trump's inauguration crowd size, 'We have alternative facts.'

These constant and unyielding garden variety lies are a heinous enough quality in a president, but what of the full text of the Ninth Holy Commandment? It is often interpreted in modern English as, 'Thou shalt not lie.' Specifically though, when Moses brought the tablets down from the mountain, the second-last item was, 'Thou shalt not bear false witness against thy neighbor.' This particular type of lie is the basis on which the president's political career was built: Trump championed the conspiracy-laden slander known as Birtherism, and it is what made him the, ahem, man he is today.

For those who missed it, Birtherism was the very definition of 'false witness against one's neighbor'. It focuses on Trump's predecessor and the first successful president in whose shadow he constantly walks, Barack Hussein Obama. The crux of the rumor was that President Obama was born in his father's native Kenya, not his native Hawaii (of course, he's black, right?) and was therefore ineligible to be president as the constitution requires a 'natural born' United States citizen. Demands to see

Obama's birth certificate were made by several prominent Republicans as well as a host of time-wasting bloggers pundits and right-wing talk show hosts (including later Medal of Freedom winner, Rush Limbaugh), hence those accusing Obama became known as 'birthers'. The idea persists today in the minds of many millions of Americans, thanks to the protracted season of smearing that Obama endured while running for a second term. Trump was at the forefront of that campaign.

At first, it would have been hard to imagine the rumor had any legs. Its beginnings were inauspicious. As early as 2004 when Obama was a rising star in the senate, a middle name like Hussein didn't help: it was the name of Iraq's recently executed dictator – a sinister, Arabic-sounding name, at least to the kind of people who flip out over foreign names. He was named so because his father, had been a Muslim before eventually leaving the religion. Despite the fringe nature of the claim, 'conservative' websites picked up the rumor and ran with it in early 2008 when Obama was campaigning for president. Some supporters of Obama's Democratic primary rival Hillary Clinton circulated the rumor as well.

Yet in an increasingly polarized American political climate, where each side deeply distrusts the other and looks for any opportunity for a cheap shot, the rumor picked up steam surprisingly quickly, especially among Republicans looking to make a racial attack without calling it race. Before long, prominent right-wing radio hosts such as Rush Limbaugh were demanding Obama publicly release his birth certificate, and even a Democratic committee member from Pennsylvania brought a lawsuit against Obama demanding the same. The calls were dismissed, Obama won the election and the rumor went quiet until the following cycle – the campaign for re-election in 2012.

By this time the internet rumor-mill was much more sophisticated, and the birther conspiracy quickly spread to millions more subscribers via blogs, websites and powerful social media platforms such as Facebook. Pressed by their white, right-wing base, Republican leaders and conservative voices raised the hue and cry again about this colored interloper, demanding answers to the 'question' of Obama's birthplace. A rogue's gallery of right-wing favorites such as serial adulterer and former House Speaker Newt Gingrich, Alabama senate candidate and suspected child Molester Roy Moore, conspiracy theorist and one-time vice presidential candidate Sarah Palin, Arizona sheriff and convicted criminal Joe Arpaio, religious whackos such as Michelle Bachman and Mike Huckabee, all jumped on the bandwagon along with the usual line-up of firebrand TV and radio voices including Fox's Sean Hannity, conspiracy-theorist and champion campaigner against the Lizard People, Alex Jones (look it up), and talk radio's Rush Limbaugh again. Before long it was a national scandal but still characterized by disparate voices and in need of a unifying figurehead. That leadership would come from stern TV reality host, beauty pageant organizer and aspiring presidential candidate Donald J. Trump.

Trump eagerly placed himself at the center of this manufactured controversy. The conman instinct sensed early on that a large portion of the Republican base was suspicious of the potential first black president and that vein of bigotry could be exploited. He quickly added his own embellishments to the bearing of false witness against Obama, with such easily disproven claims as 'Growing up nobody knew him,' and 'There is something on that birth certificate he doesn't like.' Trump assured viewers he had dispatched private investigators to Obama's official birthplace of Honolulu to follow up: not much was heard after the announcement, likely because they found nothing of significance or more likely, Trump had never sent anyone in the first place. One can only hope at least these gumshoes got a nice beach holiday on Trump's dime. He did the rounds on TV, talk radio and in a friendly tabloid newspaper the National Inquirer insisting he would 'get to the bottom of this.'

This became the foundation of Trump's political brand and he took it on a roadshow across the country. He appeared on late-night talk shows, radio programs, built a website and repeated the claim in speech after speech. For several months Donald Trump was the toupee-wearing, orange-skinned face of birtherism. He claimed that Obama's Columbia university ID stated he was a 'foreign student,' that Obama had spent over $2 million in legal fees trying to conceal the fact (he hadn't spent a dime), that his grandmother in Kenya claimed to have witnessed his birth there, that his alleged classmates at school and university 'never saw him,' and after being caught, that Hillary Clinton herself began the movement: 'she was all in.' These steps are typical of Trump's pattern of lying: grab a rumor (or make one up), when challenged lie bigger, and bigger still and when you finally get caught, blame someone else.

When Obama finally got tired of what he characterized in one speech as 'this silliness' and released his official birth certificate in 2011, it didn't quite shut Donald up. Instead, Trump claimed credit for forcing Obama to release the certificate and putting the controversy to rest. Though he must have suffered some degree of public humiliation – the man without shame still hates to lose – Trump's just desserts arrived at the annual White House correspondents' dinner to which he'd been invited and which he attended, only to be teased by the then-president, in the light-hearted spirit of the evening, for pursuing conspiracy theories and foolish rumors. In the video he grimaced, visibly uncomfortable, while a room full of celebrities laughed on. Many suspected that the reason Trump has made it his mission to undo all Obama has done stems from this moment, though it will be remembered he targeted Obama from the start with his embrace of this racist origin theory. It was not until 2016 and his own serious presidential run that Trump admitted Obama was not born in Kenya, and even then with a shrug and a mutter.

But since there was little merit to the accusation, to begin with – as the child of an American mother it wouldn't have mattered if Obama had been born overseas, he'd still be a natural-born American – why did Trump pursue it? After all Obama's 2008 presidential opponent John McCain was born on a US base in Panama and there was no nationwide movement to expose his birth certificate. Of course, McCain was white. Again the mere accusation was enough. It tapped that current of white rage at the liberals, coastal elites, intellectuals and minorities and Obama was all of these to them. It pandered to the belief a black man could not lead the country, or indeed that people of color were inferior and could not truly be called American. It stoked the fear of a Muslim-sounding name.

Trump carried forward this theme of racial animus when his own campaign was launched in earnest. He descended the tacky, gilded escalators of his own gaudy hotel and declared immigration to be his number one concern. Mexicans were drug dealers and rapists and eventually, that would metastasize into his calls for an improbable border wall and a ban on Muslims. However the faithful were already converted as if they had needed much convincing. They hated foreigners, people of color and were more than ready to vote for a man who stood up for what they saw as 'real' American values. Disregarding Christ's exhortations to 'love thy neighbor as thyself,' Trump has continued throughout his presidency to rail against asylum seekers, Muslims, undocumented migrants, and African

American cities and communities: Baltimore was 'rat-infested' and again that people fleeing poverty and violence in Haiti or West Africa come from 'shithole countries.' Though often stymied in the courts, Trump persists in signing orders and bills that restrict the arrival of people from poor, brown, religiously different parts of the world. The premise of hating foreigners that began with the birther conspiracy has become a hallmark of the Trump presidency and a crowd-favorite among his red hat-sporting base.

Trump has made it a habit of lying about more recent enemies as well. The team that investigated him for potential collusion with Russian spies during the 2016 election was frequently derided in midnight tweets as 'twelve angry Democrats,' when in fact the majority of them were lifelong Republicans. He had a field day with Hillary Clinton and the allegations that she had been responsible for the Benghazi debacle, where a Libyan militia assault on a US embassy resulted in several American deaths. As discussed, he has insisted there is some sort of corruption scandal involving the Bidens, Ukrainian gas firm Burisma, and also Crowdstrike, a US-based internet security firm that allegedly influenced the 2016 election but for which he has provided exactly zero evidence.

There are enemies within as well: when advisers leave his side, such as former generals Mattis and Kelly, Secretary of State Rex Tillerson or National Security adviser John Bolton, men he once praised as stand up guys become 'Never Trumpers,' a mildly derisive term used to describe Republicans who had opposed Trump's candidacy to begin with. His former campaign adviser Steve Bannon earned the nickname 'Sloppy Steve' after criticizing Trump's intellectual capacity; he called Jim Mattis, former Defense Secretary, 'the world's most overrated General'. In short, Trump has no problem breaking the ninth commandment and lying about everyone around him.

The lies came back to bite between 2022 and 2024 when former president Trump went on civil and criminal trial in New York for defamation and falsifying records. First, he was found liable for defamation against E. Jean Carroll, the woman who accused him of sexual assault in the plush Bergdorf Goodman Department store. The accusations arose later around the time of the Me Too movement, that sank the careers of wealthy sex predators such as Harvey Weinstein and Jeffrey Epstein. Trump accused Carroll of being a liar and the accusations of being politically motivated, so she took him to court. She won $5 million in damages, and Trump slandered her again immediately after so she took him back to court, this time getting an $83 million award. In the second trial, the jury also found Carroll's accusations of sexual assault to be credible. Among the evidence, Trump's own words on the famous 'Access Hollywood' tape (see Chapter Seven) where he bragged about sexual assault, describing almost exactly the details of Carroll's accusation.

Then, for Trump's New York property empire where he and his lawyers inflated property values and even square footage to secure loans, then shrunk them again when it was time to declare assets for tax purposes. In one example, Trump's own three-storey residence in Fifth Avenue's Trump Tower was first listed as 11,000 square feet, ballooned to 30,000 for a loan security and mysteriously shrunk again when it was tax time. Trump's accountant admitted the value had been overstated by 'Give or take $200 million'. In early 2024 the judge ordered the Trump organization to pay over $400 million in penalties. During the trial, Trump and his legal team also dithered on delivering subpoenaed documents and dabbled in frivolous challenges, earning tens of thousands more in penalties for contempt of court.

In the famous Stormy Daniels case, a jury found in 2024 that Mr. Trump had indeed paid money to the adult film actress of that screen name, then misrepresented the payments as business expenses. The affair took place in the mid 2000s while Trump was married to his third wife, but the hush money came ten years later when Trump was running for president, along with a Non Disclosure Agreement. There was nothing illegal about cheating on his wife and paying the other woman to be silent but the State argued the money was an election expense because the timing demonstrated it was to protect his reputation while he ran for office, not his marriage. Trump had his lawyer Michael Cohen pay Daniels $130,000 for her silence in 2016 then reimbursed the lawyer in several dozen installments running into 2017, during his first few months in the Oval Office. By claiming this as a normal legal expense and not a campaign expense, Trump had broken the law and was found guilty on all 34 counts. Sentencing has been scheduled for September 2024, just before his next potential election.

Trump's grandest and most enduring falsehood has proven his most successful. It has kept seventy million rabid supporters by his side, fuelled donations for his reelection and to cover his enormous legal bills and ensured he remained firmly in the media spotlight between his 2020 election loss and his second run in 2024. This is the lie that the 2020 election was stolen, that Joe Biden and the democrats somehow cheated, and that Trump remains the rightful President of the United States, even after leaving office. This has come to be known as simply 'The Big Lie.'

The campaign to steal the 2020 results was deeply tied to its marketing push. Trump and his surrogates claimed many times before, during and since that the election had been rigged from the start. This was vital repetition – Goebbels style – to reinforce the idea in the minds of his supporters and give a veneer of legitimacy to the very illegal acts the President subsequently committed in his attempt to thwart the democratic process (see Chapter Eight). These included a media blitz by Trump and spokespersons, pressuring officials to play along and repeat the lie and even a raft of frivolous and ultimately doomed lawsuits purportedly challenging the results. Finally, the lie has been repeated as often as possible since the election to continue to generate enthusiasm and revenue and keep Donald Trump in the spotlight.

By the time the 2016 election rolled around, Trump had repeated the claim that it was rigged against him dozens of times. By the 2020 election season it may have been hundreds; by 2024, hundreds more. It has become a central pillar of his candidacy and an article of faith among his followers. In 2016 even after winning, Trump held that there was rampant fraud because he lost the popular vote, saying, 'I won the popular vote if you deduct the millions of people who voted illegally,' and claiming that several million 'illegal immigrants' voted for Hillary Clinton.

There was never any evidence an election fraud commission created by Trump after taking office found none. In 2018's midterm elections, Trump cried, 'Law Enforcement has been strongly notified to watch closely for any ILLEGAL VOTING which may take place in Tuesday's Election (or Early Voting).' Despite early voting being perfectly legal and regulated. In 2020 Trump added, 'the only way we're going to lose this election is if the election is rigged.' And after his loss, 'This is a fraud on the American public. This is an embarrassment to our country.

We were getting ready to win this election. Frankly, we did win this election.'

So important has The Big Lie become that those who were once targets of the claim have embraced it. Ted Cruz, a primary rival of Trump's in 2016 complained at the time, 'Apparently, when anyone votes against him, it's an act of theft.' Cruz endorsed Trump after losing the primary in 20216 and even went to work on the phones to solicit donations after Trump had famously insulted his wife's looks. In 2021 after Trump lost and cried foul, Cruz claimed, 'For those who respect the voters, simply telling the voters, 'Go jump in a lake, the fact that you have deep concerns is of no moment to us' that jeopardizes, I believe, the legitimacy of this and subsequent elections.'

To back this up, a legion of supporters online and on the airwaves created a tapestry of fantasies to 'prove' the election was stolen. Election officials who refused to comply with the Trump Campaign's pressure to overturn the count were denounced as Democratic operatives, even those who were Republicans. Grainy video footage was released of county election officials in key battleground states where Trump lost moving boxes, tallying votes and in some cases taking out the trash, all with scary music, baritone voice-overs and subtitles suggesting something nefarious was going on without offering any proof. This has led to death threats and lawsuits against election officials and staffers of both parties in Georgia, Arizona and Michigan among others.

Though some of the conspiracy theories were spontaneous, created by imaginative online trolls or Russian propaganda sites, much of this campaign of disinformation was directed from the top down. According to the indictments Trump instructed his subordinates to disseminate these falsehoods, constituting a criminal act. Some complied out of loyalty to the cause. Some, conservatives but not cultists, demurred. Others practically told him to go fuck himself.

Rudy Giuliani was an easy mark. For whatever reason the former New York Mayor and conservative hero from 9/11 decided to hitch his wagon to Trump. He campaigned heavily for the president and was instrumental in fundraisers. He was right there at the party on election night, reportedly very drunk, claiming loudly that they had won. He led many of the president's lawsuits to overturn the numbers. He also pressured officials and slandered election workers in pursuit of a recount. Giuliani's post-election antics veered between the criminal and the farcical: before being later indicted in Georgia and Arizona for election interference, he held a 'Stop the Steal' press conference in a run-down parking lot outside a landscaping warehouse situated beside a dildo shop to decry the alleged elected fraud of 2020. Giuliani thought he had booked the Four Seasons Hotel but got a gardening firm of the same name instead.

As the failed legal challenges mounted, Trump believed he could use the power of his office and the state apparatus to ram through a revision regardless. This later underpinned his defense in his criminal trials that a president has full immunity for executing his responsibilities in office. Many of his top advisors did not agree that denying an election result constituted an official act. Trump pressured Attorney General Bill Barr to open a Department of Justice Investigation into the election results to lend credibility to this denial. A longtime supporter, but also a man who knew the law, Barr resigned, rather than become part of a criminal conspiracy. When Trump was impeached a second time, shortly before leaving office and this time for attempting to steal the election, Barr testified, 'I made it clear I did not agree with the idea of saying the election was stolen and putting out this stuff which I told the president was bullshit. I didn't want to be a part of it and that's one of the reasons I decided to leave when I did.'

Barr's replacement, Acting AG Richard Donoghue was no more receptive. While Trump insisted on pursuing the internet rumors of stuffed ballot boxes, tossed ballots and other nefarious acts alleged in grainy video footage, Donoghue told him, 'The major allegations are not supported by the evidence developed. We've looked in Georgia, Pennsylvania, Michigan, Nevada. Much of the info you're getting is false.' Campaign manager Bill Stepien advised Trump not to declare victory on the night, but his boss went ahead anyway with his infamous 'frankly we did win' claim. Later in November as Trump pursued court cases and demanded recounts, Stepien described his chances as 'Very, very bleak'.

Campaign Lawyer Alex Cannon also informed his bosses that they were unlikely to scratch a win out of recounts and fraud allegations. He suggested Trump's trade advisor Peter Navarro promoted conspiracies of widespread fraud and said Navarro dismissed a Cybersecurity and Infrastructure Security Agency report that found the election had been very secure. 'I believe Mr. Navarro accused me of being an agent of the deep state working against the president.' Trump's own daughter and top advisor Ivanka also sided with AG Barr, testifying, 'It affected my perspective. I respect Attorney General Barr, so I accepted what he was saying.'

So while many at the top knew privately that Trump's push to overturn the election was going nowhere, he and his campaign continued a public relations and litigation putsch to either secure the recounts he wanted or at least convince enough of his supporters out there that they had been robbed somehow. The lawsuits were a colossal failure. A total of sixty suits were brought in seven swing states by the Trump campaign, affiliated PACs or supporters. Of the sixty, exactly *one* case was ruled in favor of Trump over some procedural details. Procedure was not generally the campaign's strong point however as over a dozen of the cases filed in Georgia, Wisconsin, Arizona, Michigan, New Mexico, Pennsylvania and DC were tossed due to incorrect filing and other errors. Thirty-three more cases were dismissed due to lack of evidence and another fourteen dropped by the plaintiffs when it became clear they wouldn't win.

Many of Joe Biden's 2020 Electoral College wins were achieved with razor-thin margins. Arizona and Georgia it came down to a little over 10,000 ballots in key urban areas. In Wisconsin, he won by only 20,000 votes out of millions cast. The Trump campaign claimed falsely that Wisconsin had paused the counting once it had found enough votes for Biden and that later 100,000 uncounted ballots had been discovered. As in other states, Trump's campaign challenged absentee voting and mail-in ballots, having claimed since before the election that these were ripe targets for fraud, despite there being no empirical evidence to support the claim. They wanted those ballots struck off and as with other states they only challenged in the counties where Trump lost. In its ruling against the Trump campaign, the Wisconsin Supreme Court wrote, 'Striking these votes now — after the election, and in only two of Wisconsin's 72 counties when the disputed practices were followed by hundreds of thousands of absentee voters statewide — would be an extraordinary step for this court to take. We will not do so.'

It is not likely the Trump campaign ever truly expected to win these lawsuits. It was just for show, to run cover for the Big Lie and give it an air of legitimacy. If the nation could be convinced something fishy was going on, it might tolerate the President's heavy-handed measures to stamp it out. Many did believe the claims and they showed up in force on January 6,

2021. As explained in chapters six and eight, after a brief speech from Trump, they proceeded to storm the Capitol, smashing windows, overturning furniture, stealing property, assaulting cops and smearing feces on the walls.

This was all done because Trump lied. He got up on the podium that day, repeated the claim the election had been stolen, exhorted Vice President Mike Pence to 'do the right thing' and shirk his constitutional duty to certify the result. He also promised to march on the Capitol with the angry mob he had fired up over the previous two months and past several hours. These were all lies. It had by then been roundly disproved in sixty different lawsuits; Mike Pence ignored Trump's demands and did the actual 'right thing' and certified the election count, and Donald Trump most certainly did not join the riot he encouraged, instead hiding out in the White House and watching the carnage on TV. Two weeks later on January 20, the mess was cleaned up and under tight security, Joe Biden was driven to the Capitol where he was sworn in as 46th President. Donald Trump did not attend the inauguration.

The Big Lie not only drove the violence of January 6, it has been Trump's stock-in-trade since losing the election. He repeats it at rallies and campaign speeches. He tweets it and posts it on his own social media site Truth Social. It is sent in direct mails soliciting donations and appears on his web pages where people go to make those donations. His surrogates in the media such as Sean Hannity and Tucker Carlson on Fox News, Breitbart's

Steve Bannon and disgraced web host Alex Jones have continued to repeat allegations (Fox news was forced to pay *over a billion dollars* in reparations after defaming the manufacturer of many voting machines, claiming they had deliberately tampered with the numbers. This was finally enough to get Carlson fired). Election denials and conspiracies have been posted and reposted all over the internet and YouTube over the past four years and have solidified in the popular memory – at least among Republicans.

This lie has also caused a form of mass delusion. Certainly, most of Trump's supporters blindly follow his claims, but the mantra of a stolen election has become so ingrained, that Republican candidates for office up and down the country have been forced to line up and commit to it lest they offend Trump's voting base. By 2022 election deniers had become so mainstream nearly 200 Republican nominees for the mid-term elections were claiming the last election had been stolen. Worse still, by the 2024 election season, election deniers had wormed their way into positions of power where they may be able to influence the outcome of the election. Officials who had promoted election conspiracy theories were identified in at least 16 counties in six swing states: Arizona, Georgia, Michigan, Nevada, North Carolina, and Pennsylvania. It is not hard to imagine these officials tampering with voting machines; they might seek to stop the counting when it starts to go against them; they may seek lawsuits for recounts or - to even toss batches of votes – they tried to do all this in 2020. Only this time they won't be lobbying from the outside with Rudy Giuliani: they will be in a position to do it themselves, with state and county resources and the authority of their own offices. Two dozen of them have already refused or delayed certification in recent years.

Bearing false witness against Barack Obama launched Trump's political career. Without this particular lie, Trump may not have built the cult-like following that energized his 2016 campaign and propelled him into the Oval Office. To sustain this support after his disastrous 2020 loss against Joe Biden, Trump was forced to lie bigger and concocted a grand scheme to keep tens of millions of supporters believing the election had been stolen from him – many of whom reacted violently on January 6, 2021. By tapping this vein of white rage, a guy from a TV show with funny hair positioned himself the champion of White America. This was the lie that enabled all the others as if Trump needs an excuse to lie Trump may have been motivated by one other factor and one that Obama's presidency and later Biden's most certainly aggravated, but also one that Trump has likely suffered from his entire life: that little green demon, envy.

10. THOU SHALT NOT COVET

'Is it wrong to be more sexually attracted to your own daughter than your wife?'

- Perversions, 6:18

Donald Trump is a deeply insecure man. Despite being born with a silver spoon and having every advantage growing up, he is envious of just about everyone. He is jealous of the genuinely successful, the real self-made men; of those wealthier, more popular, better-looking and more youthful; the more politically successful and critically acclaimed – just about everyone, and it shows when he brags and belittles in his speeches and tweets. He covets what others have, from Nobel prizes to his name in lights. It will be noted from the first couple of chapters in this book that the only time Trump ever saw his name in lights was when he paid to have the signage put up himself. Donald J. Trump is a needy little bitch.

One 'achievement' that Trump values highly is TV ratings. As a man who has never had genuine friends he craves the attention of the masses. His reality show, The Apprentice, in which candidates vied to win the mogul's approval to run one of his 'businesses,' did alright for a while. However, after fourteen seasons the format had grown somewhat stale. Trump was replaced as star and host by tough-guy actor and former California governor, Arnold Schwarzenegger but by then the show's ratings were already reportedly taking a hit from name-association with the toxic xenophobia of Trump's presidential campaign. When the show wrapped up early because even the Austrian Oak had been unable to keep it afloat, the new president couldn't resist tweeting about it gleefully: 'He was fired by his bad (pathetic) ratings, not by me. Sad end to great show.' Since then, whenever Schwarzenegger has ripped Trump about his bigotry, human rights record or political corruption scandals, Trump jabbed back not about the topics at hand, but about the show ratings, revealing the depth of his understanding of politics. The bigger man, Schwarzenegger was able to look at the bigger picture: when discussing why people still want to come to America even in the age of Trump, the Austrian immigrant said it was, 'Because they know that one president, one man, cannot change this country.'

Trump's Twitter following, now very large by any measure at around 60 million members, was also a constant point of insecurity for him. Early in the campaign when he could boast a healthy ten million followers, of those ten it was estimated at the time that around 4 million were bots – fake accounts set by an algorithm to 'behave' like people, posting preset comments and sharing popular tweets with genuine users and other bots. This gave the illusion Trump had more traffic than he really did (his opponent Hillary Clinton had a similar number of bots at the time). At the time however, The Donald was not satisfied with six million real followers and four million fake ones: he bragged that his pool of Twitter fans stood at 22 million.

Trump has proven similarly obsessed with the economy. Of course he has never had the patience for real measures such as quality of living and social mobility: instead mere numbers will suffice, such as the stock indices and the raw number of jobs created (ignoring those lost where possible).

The stock market seems to be a gauge Trump puts much value on, especially since he likely owns millions of shares and his wealthy supporters reap similar dividends when he cuts taxes and the Dow climbs. Despite dire warnings from economists that the share market is always overbought before a crash; disregarding the dangerously long winning streak of Wall Street investors, not to mention that the market has been climbing since several years before Trump became president, he seems to take personal pride in the Dow's successes. Trump's first stock boast came only six weeks after his election a tellingly, six weeks before he even took office, noting the Dow was up 10% and boldly claiming, 'The world was gloomy before I won - there was no hope.' Even though the trend began under Obama and has merely continued, every point higher is a point Trump's predecessor 'failed' to achieve and therefore a sign of his own greatness. 'If the Dems (Crooked Hillary) got elected, your stocks would be down 50% from values on Election Day. Now they have a great future - and just beginning!' At least in part the tax cuts he offered to the rich resulted in billions in stock buybacks, bolstering the market and sending indices higher. Trump tweets, 'Dow goes from 18,589 on November 9, 2016, to 25,075 today, for a new all-time Record. Jumped 1000 points in last 5 weeks, Record fastest 1000 point move in history. This is all about the Make America Great Again agenda! Jobs, Jobs, Jobs. Six trillion dollars in value created!' He may have been gearing up to remind us of his stock market 'success' when he tweeted late one night, 'Despite the constant negative press covfefe…' and left it at that. We'll never know.

In line with boasts made about his daughter's magical job-creating skills, Trump also believes he alone has saved employment from the abyss. Taking just one demographic, African Americans, the unemployment rate has been declining for a decade, making it difficult to lay all this success at the feet of the most recent president. It is also a mixed blessing, as job growth itself has done little to improve the wages or living conditions of everyday Americans. Trump tweeted, 'So if African-American unemployment is now at the lowest number in history, median income the highest, and you then add all of the other things I have done, how do Democrats, who have done NOTHING for African-Americans but TALK, win the Black Vote?'

This is the same man who claimed those in black neighborhoods are living in 'hell,' berated African American congressman Elijah Cummings for representing 'rat-infested'

Baltimore, who referred to Haitian and Caribbean refugees of African descent as people coming from 'shithole countries,' and who challenged the first black president on whether he could even call himself American. It is hard to imagine why he would be so jealous of the Democratic party's success with black voters.

Trump's business achievements and property development are also a sign of this covetous insecurity. His desire to license his name to everything and put the golden letters TRUMP atop the highest tower in every city reeks of a toy poodle trying to pee as high up the post as it can. When he proved spectacularly poor at actually developing property, with deals falling through and contractors getting screwed, Trump became content to license his name to other builders so he could ride their coattails to the top. Not content at having his gaudy signature splashed – like poodle piss – all over town, Trump felt burned when his buildings weren't the tallest. He was vindicated when the twin towers of the World Trade Center collapsed in the September 11 terror attack: with touching display of empathy, Trump bragged in a talk radio interview later that very day that his building at 40 Wall Street, 'became known as the second tallest and now it's the tallest.'

Not only does Trump love to measure substitute phalluses, on the 2016 campaign trail he publicly bragged about his actual penis size. Taking umbrage at any slight, including the juvenile rumor that his hands are unusually small, he jabbed back at

Republican primary rival Marco Rubio who had teased him in a live televised debate. When Rubio suggested small hands meant a small something else, the future president reassured the debate audience and millions of TV viewers, 'Look at these hands, are they small hands? If they're small, something else must be small. I guarantee you there's no problem, I guarantee.' According to Stormy Daniels, the adult film star Trump slept with apparently there is: she likened the appendage to a 'toadstool' on late-night talk TV.

Trump's desire to put his name on everything then sell it is also a sign of deep-seated envy. He just cannot stand the idea that his name might not be on everyone's lips and seeks to monetize it where he can with cheap, licensed paraphernalia. Hawking an autographed bible ($59) might be the most egregious example because it breaks the Third Commandment, but especially since he left office and has faced ballooning legal costs, there seems to be no limit to the varieties of junk he sells to his supporters.

These form part of a broader scam to bilk his fans of their money as much as to satisfy his ego, but it must be stressed a fool and his money are easily parted and they do pay willingly. Among the items Trump has sold through his various websites and online outlets are sneakers for $399, commemorative two-dollar bills featuring his mug shot from the Georgia indictment at $20 and the chance for donors to put their names on his new plane, costing up to $2,500, recurring monthly. He has offered new limited edition sneakers featuring his post-assassination attempt fist-pump image for $299; a series of non-fungible tokens at $99 a pop, and shares in his Truth Social media company, which fell from $64 to $29 within a week or two after the IPO and are still dropping like a stone.

The NFTs seem especially egregious because savvy day traders could at least short the stock and make money off Trump's loss. But with the Tokens you get literally nothing. NFTs are a new form of 'art' made up mostly of digitally generated images and animations that are supposed to be unique. Some have been bought and sold for millions. Trump's offering however could hardly be called unique.

They appeared to be a series of online trading cards featuring AI-generated images of Trump in various costumes and poses There's a muscular construction worker Trump in a yellow hard hat and another exactly the same with a white helmet. There's one with a red high-visibility vest and one in orange. You can get superhero Trump in a blue cape, or green or yellow or red, or how about soldier Trump in jungle camouflage on a forest background and soldier Trump in desert fatigues on a tan background - all exactly the same face, same pose, same sleazy grin. These were just some of the hundreds of minor variations of the same few dozen images.

The digital cards sold out quickly among his followers, but lost value almost immediately. Unfazed, Trump offered a special package a few weeks later of 47 cards (reflecting his aim to be the 47th president if he wins in 2024) bundled with an autographed scrap of the suit he wore when his mug shot was taken for the Georgia indictment. In the end anything with Trump's name on it just doesn't look like a decent investment: a billionaire who has to tap his donors for legal funds, who asks them to pay for his new private jet, and sells worthless junk for a hundred dollars each may not actually be the billionaire he makes out. Donald Trump is a grifter who covets your money.

Other targets of Trump's covetousness are again, the leaders he wishes he could be, starting with Nobel Prize winner, Iran dealmaker, the man on whose watch the economy recovered from the collapse of the housing market: the considerably more popular Barack Obama.

On day one, when he was inaugurated president, Trump boasted in his typical hyperbole of, 'the biggest inauguration crowds ever'. Estimates put Trump's crowd size at up to 600,000. This is a respectable number to turn out in Washington D.C. on a cold January day, and it is higher than George W. Bush's inaugural attendance which maxed out at 500,000 for his second term. However, it is far short of Bill Clinton's initial 800,000 and only a third of the estimated 1.8 million who attended Barack Obama's first inauguration (his second was around 1 million). Photo comparisons of people crowding the National Mall in front of the Capitol show that turnout for

Obama thronged the giant square, filling all its blocks, whereas Trump's crowd was more scattered and ended sooner, several blocks from the Capitol. Documents released under the Freedom of Information Act show Trump's solution was to have his photography team doctor the official aerial picture, cutting off the more distant, emptier sections and focusing on the crowds nearest the front.

Trump surely knows that deep down he is not and will likely never be as popular as his predecessor. The day he won the election he was even less popular than his opponent, who despite not picking up as many districts as Trump, certainly pulled in more overall votes. In fact, Trump remains the least popular president ever – at least since official polling began – with his overall score stuck permanently in the forties. Compared to other presidents, this is abysmal. Obama began his term at 67%, while Trump Started at 45% and has never reached that overall number since. Trump averaged 40% throughout his first term compared to Obama's 47% and Bush's 49%; Clinton's stands at 55% and Reagan's at 60%. Perhaps because of the base rallies around an impeached president, Trump saw a spike to about 44% at the start of his Senate trial and by some measures 49% at the end. Bill Clinton's post-impeachment approval was 73%.

Trump could be forgiven for thinking he is more popular than he really is. Even after the 2020 election, which he lost by more than eight million votes, he still gathered about 72 million.

Moreover they are well spread across most states. When he plays to packed-out auditoriums of the most faithful he must feel like a rock star. Perhaps this is what prompted him to boast in 2018 he had a whopping 75% support. The same year he also tweeted he had 'better numbers than Obama at this point,' which was only partly true: a little over a year into his presidency, Obama's ratings on the economy had dipped as the country struggled with a financial crisis that had started just before he took office, yet his score on healthcare and other issues was still better than Trump's. Even among his own party, where he holds higher support, Trump could not help embellishing. When 80% of registered Republicans supported him in late 2019, he cherry-picked a Zogby Poll that put it ten points higher than the aggregate of other more reliable pollsters. Then he added another four points out of thin air, claiming 94 percent. Mr. Trump's insecurity and mathematical prowess intersect in the telling comment he made in March of 2018: 'Whatever they say Trump's poll numbers are, add nine.'

Of Obama's achievements, the 45th president seems particularly jealous. Partly perhaps as revenge for one-upping him with facts on the birther controversy, perhaps just for being a black president, Trump has delighted in undoing laws Obama's administration managed to get passed. Environmental regulations that combat global warming and protect Americans from pollution have been rolled back; national parks and reservations protected for decades have been opened to oil and gas exploration. Clean air and water standards have been eroded; Obama's expanded health coverage including provisions for those with pre-existing conditions has been vigorously undermined; a deal to stop Iran enriching weapons-grade uranium unilaterally abandoned and America has been withdrawn from the Paris Climate Accord. Every effort Obama made to leave the nation and the world a better place has been sabotaged by his replacement in favor of big businesses, obsolete industries, hawkish posturing or just for nihilistic kicks.

But the one achievement Trump cannot undo is also the one he is never likely to get because he cannot take it himself: the Nobel Peace Prize. This is because one has to work very hard or inspire others, improve the world and make things better for millions, whereas Trump is a spiteful, mean bastard who has never helped anyone in his life.

The ink had barely dried on the 2008 ballot papers when the Nobel Committee awarded President-elect Obama the prize: he hadn't even begun his first term. The spokesperson made it clear it was not so much for what Obama had done – merely winning an election and having made promises he was yet to be tested on – but because of what he might do. It was hoped the first African American president could heal the racial divides, improve the lives of minorities and aspire to a better, more inclusive united states, and indeed the world. It was in other words, an aspiration, and it was made clear from the start that Obama would be expected to earn it. However right-wing bloggers, radio hosts, columnists, and TV presenters pounced on the award, ridiculing the Nobel Committee for granting an award to Obama 'just for being black.' Trump later complained that the selection process was 'rigged' against him and that Obama 'had no idea why he got it.'

Trump has lashed out against other do-gooders as well, suggesting he should have gotten the prize instead. The most prominent of these little award spats was against Greta Thunberg, the Swedish teenager who sailed solo around the world raising awareness of the dangers of climate change. When she was placed on the cover of TIME magazine, as its Person of the Year, Conservatives argued that a teenage girl deserves the award far less than the many researchers and scientists who have spent a lifetime gathering data and raising the alarm. Observers will note this thereby undermines their own default stance that climate change is a hoax. Right-wing pundits and writers were quick to dismiss Thunberg as hopelessly naive and Trump promptly joined the chorus of old, privileged white men visibly threatened by an adolescent, tweeting that the young activist needed to 'work on her anger management problem.' He retweeted an image of the TIME cover that had been doing the internet rounds, with his own head photoshopped onto Thunberg's body. Trump was also known to have custom made Time Man of the Year covers made for portraits at his properties. He also claimed in 2024 that the state of Michigan nominated him as its Man of the Year, though no such contest is held.

When Norwegian parliamentarians nominated Thunberg for a Nobel Prize in 2019, Trump must have been similarly incensed, but by then had bigger fish to fry. The Peace Prize eventually went to Ethiopia's Prime Minister for ending decades of hostility towards neighboring Eritrea. Trump claimed credit during a rally in Ohio: 'I made a deal. I saved a country, and I just heard the head of that country is now getting the Nobel Peace Prize for saving that country. Did I have something to do with it? Yeah.' The United States had not been involved in the process at all, but apparently, Trump can take credit just because he's heard of Eritrea as well.

Trump's own attempts to get nominated have been pitiful. You will recall that when he delivered his proposed peace initiative for Israel and the Palestinians, it was so one-sided that fighting immediately broke out again between the two parties. He claimed in a press conference that the Japanese Prime Minister had nominated him for his work on getting North Korea to stop sending its test missiles in their direction, but North Korea is still testing rockets. Unusually direct in its diplomacy, Japan's foreign ministry conceded that it had been asked by Washington to nominate Trump. Yes, the president actually requested a Nobel Peace Prize, the first head of state to ever do so. Given Trump's at home track record of vilifying migrant workers, deriding African immigrants, barring Muslims from entry and arresting and detaining asylum seekers, a genuine nomination sounds like an unlikely prospect; unless there's a Nobel Prize for bigotry.

More so than the praise attained by his predecessor, Trump seems to envy the iron grip of a good old-fashioned dictator. His expressed love of authoritarian rulers and attempts to emulate them must also add up to instant disqualification for any kind of peace award. He has recommended shutting newspapers down, banned reporters from press conferences and expressed interest in jailing journalists, leakers and whistleblowers, just like his idol Vladimir Putin does. Prison would not be purely for revenge: former FBI director James Comey recounted how Trump expressed interest in sending journalists to jail to 'find out what they know.' In fact, Trump wants to incarcerate a lot of people, suggesting political opponents such as rival candidate Hillary Clinton, Democratic senators and congressmen involved in his impeachment and special prosecutor Robert Mueller should all be 'locked up.' Just like any self-respecting autocrat would.

Turkey's President Recep Tayyip Erdogan – jailer of protestors and journalists – is high on the list, and Trump has claimed to be 'a great fan' of his. When Erdogan's motorcade stopped in a Washington D.C. park to beat up anti-regime protestors (and a couple of local police officers who got involved) Trump's administration allowed his thugs to leave without pressing charges. He lets foreign dictators impose their will on Americans at home, in the capital. There are at least two Trump-named buildings in Istanbul.

Of Philippine President Duterte, known for assassinating journalists and whose police hit squads have murdered hundreds of narcotics suspects, including gunning down addicts in the street, Trump has said 'Unbelievable job on the drug problem.' There is a 57-floor Trump Tower in Manila. Egypt's strongman and Trump's 'favorite dictator,' Abdel Fattah el-Sisi has 'done a fantastic job.' Trump has several businesses registered in General Sisi's country. China's Xi Xinping, known for jailing journalists, putting Uighir Muslims in concentration camps, persecuting Christians and the Falun Gong Buddhist sect and leading a nation with the world's highest execution numbers, Trump assures us is, 'a good man.' The Trump family, including daughter Ivanka has secured dozens of licensing and patent deals in China since he became president.

Regarding North Korea's third-generation tyrant, Kim Jong-Un, whose country has been called a 'Gulag State,' Trump has plenty of praise, especially on the subject of immigration: 'Nobody is trying to get into your country,' he gushed. No kidding. He has also called Kim, 'very smart,' and told him, 'I have so much to learn from you, you must be doing something right.' When a satirical website reported Trump wanted to build a new hotel in Pyongyang, internet readers unsurprisingly thought the prank was true.

The big daddy of them all though is Vladimir Putin, who is 'very much a leader' and who maintains 'strong control over a country.' Putin has outlawed homosexuality, jailed political opponents, murdered whistleblowers and journalists and shut down papers and news stations that criticize him. On journalists and reporters, Trump joked with Putin at the G20 Summit, 'Get rid of them. Fake news is a great term, isn't it? You don't have this problem in Russia but we do.' Trump has had extensive business dealings with the Russians as well, including his Miss Universe pageant, and as noted, has been trying to build a Trump Tower in Moscow for years. But more than that he would love to be free of a critical press, nosy reporters, principled whistleblowers and a meddling system of checks and balances, much the way some of his dictator buddies operate. He speaks and acts as though given the option would gladly throw his opponents – the press, Congress, election rivals – in prison or worse.

None of this will help Trump earn that 'elusive' peace prize. Yet if it is a seat in the Dictator's Hall of Fame he covets, he may be well on his way. Perhaps for the religious Right, reared on a philosophical and historical diet of obedience to an authoritarian biblical God and the mighty, heaven-sanctioned kings of the ancient near east, a strongman is just what they want. Render unto Caesar indeed.

Perhaps the one thing Trump covets above all else is women. He has been accused of forcing kisses, groping and fondling or just leering lewdly at dozens of women, some famous, some married, others barely women at all. Trump groped and put his hand up the skirt of a businesswoman on a flight where they were seated beside one another, groped an aspiring model at a nightclub and other at a dinner with business associates and a Miss USA contestant in his office. He allegedly fondled a woman standing at a taxi rank outside a tennis stadium, an Apprentice contestant, a receptionist in an elevator, a Canadian interviewer while his own wife was waiting unaware downstairs; another woman in an elevator, a Miss Universe contestant in the dressing rooms before a late-night show; at a conference at Lake Tahoe, it is claimed he propositioned another former adult film actress with $10,000 to go to his room.

It is said Trump used to burst in on beauty contestants unannounced in their changing rooms, including teen pageants. Accusers include Miss Teen Vermont, Miss Teen Wisconsin, Miss New Hampshire, Miss Arizona and Miss North Carolina, who said about her first impression of Trump, 'He eyed me like a piece of meat. I was shocked and disgusted. I have never felt so objectified…I was shocked again by this violation of our personal space. What was he doing, coming backstage when we were still getting dressed?' Don't believe them? Trump himself admitted on talk radio, 'I'm allowed to go in because I'm the owner of the pageant. And therefore I'm inspecting it…you know, they're standing there with no clothes. And you see these incredible-looking women. And so I sort of get away with things like that.'

One accuser was at a Mother's Day brunch with her husband and children at Trump's Mar-a-Largo resort, where she alleged he forced a kiss on her, in front of her family, when she tried to turn away. If non-celebrity accusers aren't your thing, you can at least take Trump's own word for it. In the famous Access Hollywood tape that broke a few weeks before his election, the future President of the United States outlined some of his favorite 'seduction' techniques, recounting the story of how he tried to woo TV personality Nancy O'Dell, confessing 'I did try to fuck her, she was married... I moved on her like a bitch. I just start kissing them, I don't even wait. When you're a star, they let you do it, you can do anything. Grab 'em by the pussy, you can do anything.'

Often when accused of sexual misconduct, The Donald has dismissed the women who've come forward as not attractive enough to warrant the attention of his tiny orange hands; or the other mushroom-sized appendage for that matter. Of Natasha Stoynoff, the Canadian journalist who accused him, Trump urged a rally audience to, 'Check out her Facebook page, then you'll understand.' After writer Jean E. Carroll accused him of sexual assault in a New York Department store Trump said, 'She's not my type.' He said of another accuser, Jessica Leeds that, 'She would not be my first choice.' However given the comments he has made about one woman in particular, perhaps we can speculate as to who that first choice might be after all: beautiful, successful, similarly-minded and unfortunately married to someone else, Trump has expressed what appears to be a sexual attraction on many occasions to his adviser, advocate, consigliore and eldest daughter, Ivanka.

Trump has a long history of making creepy statements about his own daughter, so we can be forgiven for supposing that he covets her above all the others. A quick internet search shows dozens of pictures, some candid, others staged, in which Trump can be seen posing with his daughter in a way many would describe as awkward if not suggestive. In one shot, a scantily-dressed teenaged Ivanka can be seen sitting on her father's knee and holding his face; in the same set another shot had his arm around her waist, and another with his hands on her hips. In all of these Donald can be seen smiling somewhat creepily, but then he always does that.

Another publicity picture from Ivanka's teenage years has her sitting on her father's knee again, kissing him on the cheek while one of his hands is placed firmly on the underside of her thigh. A still shot taken at a party in the nineties shows Ivanka – again dressed in skimpy attire – either getting into position on her father's knee, or getting up off it, but looks for all the world like she's in the middle of giving him a lap dance. That might be just a photo fail, but more recently, in footage of a campaign event, Trump can be seen greeting the thirty-something Ivanka with a kiss on the cheek and one hand quite awkwardly on her hip, suggestively close to her backside.

Maybe it can just be put down to a tone-deaf Donald, not really being able to anticipate what others might think, or caring much at all. After all, he hardly seems the most empathetic of people. But his own public words have led late-night comedians and news pundits alike to speculate further on his whether his interest in Ivanka is entirely paternal. Talking to radio shock jock Howard Stern in 2003, Trump boasted, 'She's got the best body. She made a lot of money as a model – a tremendous amount.' A year later on the same show, when Stern asked if he could refer to Ivanka as a nice 'piece of ass,' Trump conceded that she was. When asked on TV talk show The View whether he'd mind Ivanka posing in nude magazines, Trump responded, 'I don't think Ivanka would do that, although she does have a very nice figure. I've said if Ivanka weren't my daughter, perhaps I'd be dating her.' In another instance Trump is reported to have bragged, 'If I weren't happily married and you know, her father...' In a 2016 interview, he channeled his Access Hollywood tape when he said of his daughter that he kisses her 'with every chance I get.'

There has never been any report of actual impropriety between the two; Ivanka for her part seems devoted to her father and in interviews has been dismissive of any claims his words or actions have been inappropriate. Still, Trump has a habit of creating bad optics, and many have cringed at the photos, film footage and his own words. The Book of Exodus reads, 'Thou shalt not covet thy neighbor's house, thy neighbor's wife, nor his servants, nor his ox, nor his ass.' It hardly seems fitting for the Christian party of 'family values' to worship a man who shows so many signs he covets his daughter's ass – in the biblical context, of course. On the other hand in the Book of Genesis, God did instruct Lot's daughters to commit incest with their father, in a grubby old cave no less, so perhaps it's the sort of thing his more 'traditionalist' supporters would go in for after all.

EPILOGUE

'I take no responsibility at all'

- Covfefe 6:22

In July 2024, President Joe Biden announced he would end his campaign for reelection against Donald Trump and retire at the end of his term. Despite roundly beating Mr Trump four years earlier, Biden had run a lackluster campaign marked by questions about his age and mental fitness and at eighty-one, he was certainly looking and sounding very tired, despite a string of policy and diplomatic successes.

In their first debate of the campaign, Trump was on form, telling a whopping thirty lies according to fact checkers, on the usual subjects – immigration, abortion, guns and insults and slurs against Biden's wayward son Hunter. Biden's performance was marred by forgotten lines and missed opportunities to frame his opponent and call out falsehoods. In speeches and international conferences he mixed up the names of world leaders, much like grandpa does. The Democratic party, its donors and voters became worried and a combination of poor polling and good advice convinced Biden to end his run a month or so before receiving the formal nomination at the Democratic National Convention.

Biden immediately endorsed his VP Kamala Harris, who came out swinging. Big campaign Donors lined up behind her, pledging $200 million in the first few days and first-time small donors reached a record high by the end of the week. Harris also regained most of Biden's lost approval poll ratings within the same timeframe and gained major endorsements from party heavyweights such as Bill and Hillary Clinton and Barack and Michelle Obama, not to mention pop culture icons Taylor Swift and Beyonce Knowles. The first African American woman to receive a major presidential nomination, Harris instantly reinvigorated the campaign, especially drawing enthusiasm from the youth, women and people of color.

Only a week before his resignation, President Biden had offered kind words to Mr Trump, who had been struck and wounded by that bullet in Pennsylvania. He decried political violence, claiming it had 'No place' in America and said, 'It is a tense moment just a few days after the assassination attempt on Donald Trump, we're grateful he was not seriously injured. We continue to pray for him and his family. It's time for an important conversation in this country.'

Posting on social media, Trump's response to Biden stepping down almost as eloquent and gracious: 'Crooked Joe Biden was not fit to run for President, and is certainly not fit to serve — And never was! He only attained the position of President by lies, Fake News, and not leaving his Basement.' An hour later Trump doubled down with, 'Crooked Joe Biden is the

Worst President, by far, in the History of our Nation. He has done everything possible to destroy our Country. He was not fit to serve from the very beginning, but the people around him lied to America about his Complete and Total Mental, Physical, and Cognitive Demise.' He finished with a complaint about his suddenly less-than-favorable campaign prospects, this time with caps for emphasis: 'Crooked Joe just got knocked out, so now I'll have to do it a FOURTH TIME!!!'

Based on the Ten Commandments are the well-known and often less easily understood Seven Deadly Sins. These were originally developed by monastic desert communities in the third century but have found their way into various modern interpretations. They are pride, greed, lust, envy, gluttony, wrath and sloth. At least four of these were on display in Trump's vitriolic response to Biden, but then he has had a long history of breaking these very Christian rules as well.

Let's begin with gluttony. Though Trump avoids alcohol and sticks to drinking Diet Coke (and apparently not much else), he is known to be a fan of steaks, burgers and fried chicken (again, not much else). The Navy Doctor assigned to the White House in 2018 famously held a press conference extolling the president's health, placing his BMI conveniently – or perhaps tellingly – a few decimal points short of clinically obese at 29.1. However, Medical practitioners on social media have noted that at (allegedly) six-foot-three and 240 pounds, the president's BMI is technically 30.4, putting him neatly over the line. In any case, just looking at him he is clearly a fat bastard and a far cry from the reasonably trim playboy he had been thirty years prior. You don't get that way by eating in moderation.

On the subject of lust, this has been amply covered under his adulterousness and covetousness already but bears repeating. In a nutshell, the president cheats on his wives, pays off mistresses, offers women money for sex, sexually assaults strangers and acquaintances, walks in on women and underage girls in their changing rooms, leers at preteens, admires a known child molester for liking women 'on the younger side' and has made lustful or inappropriate comments about his own daughter. To top it all off he brags publicly about some or all of these. I think we've got him on this one.

Pride is another of the big ones, often lumped together with vanity for the sake of convenience. As we have read, Trump loves to see his name in lights, refuses to admit when he is wrong, and takes every opportunity to promote himself and where possible, to belittle others. Though he seems unconcerned about his weight, even publicly insulting women for being 'fat' (including a Miss Universe winner who had gained just a few pounds resulting in a long Twitter feud), Trump seems oblivious to his own barrel-like waistline. He is far more precious about his hairline and his tan. He clearly wears a toupee or has hair plugs, something many candid photos of a windblown comb-over handily reveal. In early 2020, Twitter erupted in laughs when a similar picture showing the white borders of his spray on-tan went viral. Trump predictably dismissed the image as 'photoshopped.' Sure, Donald.

Of the sin of greed, we have seen plenty: Trump has shown on many occasions how much he values wealth, boasting about it constantly, and his desire to acquire more. In his lifelong career of acquisitiveness, he has lied to authorities, investors and customers, cheated and underpaid contractors and creditors, dodged taxes and finally stiffed the American people, abusing the power of his office to get his way. Said Trump, 'My whole life I've been greedy ... Now I want to be greedy for the United States.' Read carefully, that could be understood a couple of ways.

The Donald also shows the classic symptoms of wrath, generally throwing toddler tantrums when he doesn't get his way and building his political brand on being angry: angry at foreigners, immigrants and the press all the time. Moreover he tapped that vein of public anger at economic disparity and white resentment at the decline of blue-collar industries to blame it all on the Muslims, the Mexicans and the Media, riding a stubborn, xenophobic wave of white rage into power. Since gaining that coveted power, he has become angrier still: with the courts for shooting down his wilder proposals, with whistleblowers and the media for exposing his wrongdoing, with Congress for acting on it. To read a Trump Tweet or watch a Trump rally speech is to witness that ball of white rage unraveling in real time. The man has very little control over his emotions.

We have witnessed how the president is guilty of sloth, being perhaps the laziest head of state in living memory. Donald Trump either cannot or will not do the job he was elected to. Though he has made some half-hearted effort to get pet projects such as his southern border 'wall' underway, he has generally neglected his duties in favor of golf trips, cable news marathons, and all-night Twitter tirades. A peep at his leaked schedule shows he works fewer hours in the day than the average American and far fewer than any previous president. For Trump, the notion of actual work formulating policy and acting on it – is best left up to a decreasing circle of nepotistic yes-men and family members, while he plays golf and goes to feel-good rallies where he can enjoy people chanting his name.

Finally, we have envy. For a man with such a massive ego, Trump seems to be awfully insecure. He has spent his life trying to win the admiration of others, to fit in with the rest of the rich list; going as far as to lie about his wealth to Forbes magazine to achieve this. He has also called in to reporters and lied about his popularity with women, claiming movie and music stars wanted to date him. As president, he has resented the electoral and policy popularity his predecessor and even what popularity the rival he defeated enjoys, and has publicly complained that he deserves more covers on TIME magazine and Nobel prizes for his so-called efforts. He may even envy his own son-in-law for being the man who was able to marry Ivanka, we will probably never know.

Though Trump has committed every one of these sins, along with breaking each of the Ten Commandments many times over, the more desperate of his evangelical base may claim that they no longer put much stock in Catholic tradition or the Old Testament (neglecting perhaps to add the caveat, 'when it's convenient') and are more focused on Christ's teachings instead. However, there's not much common ground between Trump and Jesus either.

Christ preached love, compassion and non-violence, and railed against usury and profiting from office. It is not likely he would approve of a modern US president doing all the things the ancient leaders of Judea earned his ire for. Nevertheless, evangelical leader Jerry Falwell Jr. announced, 'Mr. Trump lives a life of loving and helping others as Jesus taught in the New Testament.' Is that so Reverend?

In the Book of Mark, Jesus preaches, 'Love thy neighbor as thyself.' Trump has expressed utter disdain for his neighbors. He openly derides anyone poor, ethnic, and unconnected. In a twisted inversion of Christ's command, it is quite possible Trump loves nobody but himself. We have already seen how Trump derided black neighborhoods, slandered undocumented immigrants, attempted to block Muslims from entering the country and derided refugees merely for their country of origin.

These attacks on people of color have been a feature of his presidency and can hardly be dismissed as the odd 'gaffe.'

The plaque at the base of the Statue of Liberty asks, 'Give me your tired, your poor, your huddled masses yearning to breathe free; The wretched refuse of your teeming shore. Send these, the homeless, tempest-tossed to me,' yet Trump has made xenophobia and exclusion hallmarks of his presidency. When Asylum seekers turned up at the southern border, fleeing poverty and violence in Latin America, he had them rounded up and detained, separated from their children and kept in cages by the thousands. When such policies were challenged by a quartet of young, ethnic freshman congresswomen known as 'The Squad,' who were all black, Hispanic or Muslim, Trump responded in a twitter tirade that can only be done justice in its entirety.

Jul 15, 2019: So interesting to see 'Progressive' Democrat Congresswomen, who originally came from countries whose governments are a complete and total catastrophe, the worst, most corrupt and inept anywhere in the world (if they even have a functioning government at all), now loudly and viciously telling the people of the United States, the greatest and most powerful Nation on earth, how our government is to be run. Why don't they go back and help fix the totally broken and crime infested places from which they came. Then come back and show us how.

Three of the four congresswomen were born in the United States. These are the words of a leader supported by the

'Christian' right, whose God told them explicitly to cut that shit out. Instead, Trump has only gotten worse. When impeached and taken to trial in the senate for the high crime of trying to extort Ukraine into doing him political favors, Trump doubled down on his 'Muslim Ban,' adding half a dozen more countries (including Nigeria, which he had previously derided as place where people live in 'mud huts') to his list in order to remind his supporters he was still there and still fighting on their behalf against people of color, refugees and others from the 'huddled masses.'

The homeless, another group referred to in the Statue of Liberty plaque and another where minorities are over-represented have also been targeted. The administration proposed in 2019 an executive order banning homeless encampments and focusing on the role of law enforcement rather than any meaningful measures to combat poverty and other root causes. Among the homeless are also many veterans of America's foreign wars; some disabled, most probably traumatized, and a group that the 'conservative' Republicans, including Trump, have on many occasions pledged to support. Yet, Trump said in an interview aboard Air Force One, 'We have people living in our best highways, our best streets, our best entrances to buildings, where people in those buildings pay tremendous taxes, where they went to those locations because of the prestige. In many cases they came from other countries and they moved to Los Angeles or they moved to San Francisco because of the prestige of the city.'

As if to hammer home to the message to anyone not paying attention, in February of 2020 Trump received firebrand radio talk show host Rush Limbaugh at a solemn White House ceremony. Limbaugh had spent his career lambasting minorities and people of color, railing against programs that combat inequality and movements that promote tolerance; attacking other religions and smearing civil rights leaders. Among other things Limbaugh had suggested on his program that an African American congressman should be demoted to the role of chauffeur for the House Speaker and likened football and basketball players to gang members and 'thugs,' for speaking out against police brutality; he made fun of the way the Chinese language sounds, referred to an African American Mayor as 'massa,' suggested that Native Americans are properly compensated for their loss of life, culture, territory and livelihood by their ownership of casinos, and claimed that Spanish was the 'language of the ghetto.' Limbaugh had also loudly championed birtherism on his show.

For his efforts, Limbaugh was awarded the Presidential Medal of Freedom – the nation's highest civilian honor given to those who have made, 'an especially meritorious contribution to the security or national interests of the United States, world peace, cultural or other significant public or private endeavors.' A few days later the newly-minted Medal of Freedom winner was heard on his radio show making snide homophobic remarks about the prospect of gay presidential candidate Pete Buttigieg kissing his husband at political debates.

Christ also would have believers 'Do unto others as you would have done unto you,' but Trump has made a lifetime hobby out of whining how hard done by he is while slandering and intimidating others. Trump has claimed all manner of impropriety against his opponents – suggesting the Bidens have been involved in corrupt dealings with Ukraine, with China, while complaining loudly that impeachment proceedings against him for his own corruption were a 'witch hunt.' When insulting celebrities such as Rosie O'Donnell, whom he called 'fat,' Meryl Streep whom he called 'overrated,' Former FOX News host Megyn Kelly who is apparently 'rude and obnoxious,' he is inviting the very sort of public insult he dishes out. Yet when 2020 Democratic primary candidate and genuine self-made billionaire Michael Bloomberg ran an ad that criticized Trump for being physically out of shape, he predictably lashed out on Twitter again. To this one might add the old axiom about people in glass houses: when Bloomberg, a former New York Mayor was criticized for his controversial 'stop and frisk' law enforcement policy on the grounds it unfairly targeted minorities, Trump was quick to jump on the bandwagon. Hours later Twitter erupted with reminders that Trump himself had been a supporter of the policy at the time. The president of the United States need not be so thin-skinned about any criticism he receives – it comes with the job – yet Trump cannot help publicly responding to every slight, no matter how small.

Likewise, Trump's attempts at travel bans and other prohibitions against people entering the country fly in the face of both American tradition and his own family history. Trump has sought to ban all Muslims from entering America. This was eventually pared down to those from a list of countries which he later tried to expand. He has sought to stop asylum seekers at the border, leading to the aforementioned separations and cages; he has railed against refugees from so-called 'shithole' countries. In 2020, Trump even suggested a form of means-testing to determine whether immigrants are financially fit to remain in the country, potentially denying green cards to those who had received public financial assistance such as food stamps and other benefits. If he had gotten his way, backdated a hundred years, his own forebears might have been denied entry into the United States. Would he have liked 'others' to have done this unto his family?

The Lord also instructed us to, 'Turn the other cheek' (Matthew 5:38), yet Trump is not only a sore loser but a vindictive winner as well. This should come as no surprise as Trump has boasted publicly of his vindictiveness many more times. Repeated in another speech, the same theme: 'One of the things you should do in terms of success: If somebody hits you, you've got to hit 'em back five times harder than they ever thought possible. You've got to get even. Get even. And the reason, the reason you do, is so important…The reason you do, you have to do it, because if they do that to you, you have to leave a telltale sign that they just can't take advantage of you. It's not so much for the person, which does make you feel good, to be honest with you, I've done it many times.' Yet another iteration in a TV interview: 'If you have a problem with someone, you have to go after them. And it's not necessarily to teach that person a lesson. It's to teach all of the people that are watching a lesson.'

The 45th president went about making the entire country pay for his enmity towards Barack Obama and Hillary Clinton from day one, uprooting environmental protections, shredding foreign treaties, attempting to cut healthcare. When the Mueller probe failed to indict him, not only did Trump claim 'total exoneration' but he suggested going after the investigators in retaliation. He characterized this as 'hitting back.' In a 2009 get-rich-quick title, the future president said, 'I love getting even when I get screwed by someone. Always get even. When you are in business you need to get even with people who screw you. You need to screw them back 15 times harder. You do it not only to get the person who messed with you but also to show the others who are watching what will happen to them if they mess with you. If someone attacks you, do not hesitate. Go for the jugular.'

More recently, after the senate predictably delivered a 'not guilty' verdict at his impeachment for abuse of power and obstruction, Trump went on a purge, seeking to punish all those involved or perceived to have been. He claimed that House Speaker Nancy Pelosi had committed a crime by tearing up his State of the Union speech (she hadn't), thereby suggesting a criminal case might be made against her; he had officials who had testified unfavorably in the House hearings removed from their posts, including National Security team member Lieutenant Colonel Alexander Vindman and EU Ambassador Gordon Sondland; he had the Department of Justice open an investigation into Joe Biden's son and demanded the Treasury hand over financial documents relevant to the case. It may be recalled the entire impeachment was held over Trump's demand that Ukraine should pretend to investigate the Bidens in return for aid. Sharper observers might also note the president could have gone to the DOJ in the first place if there had been a case against Biden at all.

At a bipartisan National Prayer Breakfast and rally speeches in the days following the impeachment acquittal, Trump spent his energy railing against his enemies again, calling his detractors in the Republican Party 'dishonest' and his accusers from the Democrat side 'corrupt.' One Reverend Jefferies, leader of a Southern Baptist mega church casually dismissed the remarks: 'I think the president was completely right in what he said. It's not politically correct, but he didn't get to be president by being politically correct.' In this comment – more honest perhaps than Reverend Falwell's gushing praise – we see evangelical supporters of the president truly show their hands. They are more than happy to compromise on Christian values if it lets them hold onto power a little longer. There's more to it than just a transactional relationship as well: as much as he has become a figurehead of the white, political Right, Trump is merely a symptom, not the cause.

Abortion is considered the perennial hot button issue for Republicans and especially for the white evangelical base. While many religions hold prohibitions on terminating pregnancies, many nation-states recognize a woman's individual choice and in the separation of church and state that most democracies follow, allow believers to live their lives as they choose and non-believers to do so as well. This is effectively the cornerstone of Roe v. Wade, an early seventies Supreme Court case in which the ruling paved the way for decriminalizing abortion in the United States. Christians may argue that abortion comes under the commandment, 'Thou shalt not kill,' and is therefore tantamount to murder, but again is it really the sanctity of all human life that fires them up? They certainly show less concern over other right-to-life issues such as access to healthcare, the death penalty, the dire need of asylum seekers and refugees that largely affect people of color. Abortion, an expensive medical procedure, remains largely the 'right' of privileged white women from their own stock. In truth though, it is a relatively recent sore point in an age-old battle for the nation's heart and soul.

The animosity between the conservative American right and the forces of progress goes back centuries. They've hated each other from the start, and continued as rivals ever since, though the details and causes of spats have changed over the years (slavery was a big one). Historically both the Republican and Democratic parties have been very close to the center, diverging to such an extent only quite recently. Broadly speaking, the Republicans are seen as more homogeneous, less inclusive of minorities, more religious and socially conservative. They are also associated with big business and capitalism, with greater military spending and a more hawkish foreign policy.

The Democrats have the distinction of being known as 'socialists' though until quite recently, with the increased popularity of policies espoused by presidential candidates such as Bernie Sanders and Elizabeth Warren, they have really just been less economically right-wing than their opponents. On social issues however, the party is friendlier to minorities and the LGBT community, more inclusive of women and open to change; it certainly has broader appeal among disparate races and creeds. Yet the Democrats are often accused of being too touchy-feely, too politically correct, and 'weak' on terrorism and other external threats, real or not.

Though the parties differ on the details of many social issues, especially the roles of God, gays and guns, US foreign policy has always been pretty hawkish, no matter which side was in charge. Not a single president since the end of the Second World war hasn't sent the armed forces on some overseas adventure (Carter's Iran rescue mission was recalled because of an aircraft accident on the way), and military spending has continued to increase, largely unabated under all administrations, Republican or Democrat.

Likewise, on the international stage the United States' commitment to laissez-faire economics, interference in other countries' affairs and insistence on lofty notions of the rule of law and freedom seems to have continued independently of which party holds the reins. But domestically, ask an American who is passionate about one party or the other and he will tell you that the other is the embodiment of failure and stupidity due to a dozen points over which they appear to be diametrically opposed.

The origins of this rift could be said to have started over the civil war, the abolition of slavery and the failure of the southern Confederate States to secede. Back then, the Republican Party was headed by Abraham Lincoln, the president who emancipated African slaves and won the Civil War, forcing the South to comply – sort of – with a new spirit of egalitarianism. At that time, the Republicans were also the liberals, with such radical new ideas as freedom for black people.

The Democrats, particularly in the South, were thereafter enemies of the Republicans and of integration and equality.

Despite being forced to end slavery, they kept the 'Jim Crow' laws (so named for a famous blackface minstrel character) which ensured racial segregation in all areas of life: African Americans were no longer slaves, but they had unequal access to education, jobs, and public and private services in a version of Apartheid that endured another hundred years.

Things have changed. The Republicans are now viewed less favorably by black voters and other minorities than the democrats. In 2012, the number of African Americans identifying as Democrats was at over 70% with only 6% preferring Republicans. In the 2016 election, most surveys had the Democratic nominee Hillary Clinton beating Trump by wide margins among blacks. The first black president was a Democrat.

Though neither party can claim to be true champions of civil rights and much inequality remains, it is the Democrats who have the 'big tent': as of 2016, only 20% of African American senators and congressmen were Republicans, whereas 80% were Democrats. So how did everyone get it backwards? How is the 'Party of Lincoln' that could claim to have liberated the slaves be the one less popular with black voters? The source of today's great left-right divide is much more recent: the good old nineteen-sixties.

Ah, the sixties. Peace, love, flower power, Vietnam, civil rights, women's liberation and desegregation. On all of these the left and right fell out bloodily and after riots in the streets, arrests and a few high-profile assassinations they have never forgiven one another. The sixties saw a sexual revolution, which was anathema to religious conservatives. It saw the long and bloody military intervention in Southeast Asia which cost over 50,000 American lives, upsetting the growing peace movement. The environmental cause was beginning to pick up steam, with the inevitable pushback from big business and the political right afraid that anti-pollution regulations would affect the bottom line. And the elephant in the room, that needed clearing before all other business could be addressed was desegregation and equal rights for America's largest minority, the black community.

At this time the Southern states were still in the firm grip of the Democratic Party. Not today's 'big tent Democrats', but a narrower, deeply racist wing of the 'Good Old Boy' power network that saw whites as superior and black liberation as an existential threat. They also apparently had God on their side. Two hundred years ago the hierarchy of white men over blacks was held up as an extension of the dominion God gave man over animals in Genesis, and therefore a convenient excuse to continue capturing, keeping and trading slaves. This was an important part of the makeup of southern protestant churches. Whites did not consider blacks to be fully human or in some cases to even have souls. They argued also that biblical figures had owned slaves and so it must still be a valid concept in their own times. When owners began to introduce their slaves to

Christianity they used their religion as justification for the great crime, claiming slavery's moral virtue was that it facilitated conversion. Christian or not, racial separation was rigidly enforced, with many Christian thinkers believing miscegenation – or mixed relationships – was 'unchristian.' Even after the Civil War when African Americans were finally emancipated, churches and communities remained segregated, with very few mixed houses of worship in the South.

These states, over a dozen in all, maintained discriminatory laws that upheld segregation: black people could not eat in the same restaurants, sit in the same seats on the bus or use the same Laundromats or lavatories as whites. When Democratic President Lyndon Johnson went ahead and enforced desegregation on the southern states in the nineteen-sixties, it led to the aforementioned riots, deaths, and arrests; arson and other domestic acts of terror including the murder of key figures such as Martin Luther King. It also caused Southern Democrats to leave the party, taking their religion and its associated bigotry with them.

They did this under the banner of States' Rights – that is, the right of a state in the union to formulate its own policies without federal interference from Washington DC. In their case, they wanted to maintain the ability to deny equal rights to others. Many of these southern 'Dixiecrats' as they were known eventually migrated to the Republican party where they and their values found a home. One of President Johnson's advisors told him, 'We have just lost the South for a generation.' In fact, it has now been several generations and the Southern states, still incensed at being told they were not allowed to discriminate, have been voting fairly solidly for Republicans ever since.

The racial divide remains probably the single biggest rift between the parties. States that are overwhelmingly white are also most likely to be solidly 'red,' that is to vote for Republicans; worship of the Dixie flag and Southern heroes such as General Lee has spread to the Midwest and Northeast where populations remain mostly white as well. The 'blue' states, which tend to prefer Democrats, are usually more diverse. Race is not the only reason the two sides don't get along. Ever since the sixties, they have diverged slowly on a slew of social, economic, religious, and environmental issues, and the concept of states' rights has been harked back to whenever a (usually red) state has felt the federal government's initiatives were too disruptive or progressive for them to adopt. Their list of grievances is long and makes it somewhat horrifying to imagine what the world would be like if they got their way all the time.

On the environmental front, the liberals of the sixties and the so-called Silent Spring movement were the first to challenge big business and industry on pollution. The conservative Right has been fighting back ever since. It has devolved into fairly ludicrous battle lines, with the Republican party being the only major organization left in the world to deny climate change. They have even gone as far as to slander Rachel Carson, the environmentalist and author who kick-started modern environmentalism with her opposition to DDT and other agricultural chemicals, blaming her for the rise of malaria in Africa, due to the absence of DDT there (in fact it has always been used in fighting mosquitoes for that purpose and usage has only waned as the insects have developed immunity). To be on the Right is to be against environmentalism, which they see as a load of alarmist tree-hugging or a gateway to socialist 'cap and trade' legislation that will hinder economic progress. To be on the Right is to cling to 'macho' energy sources oil and coal and fossil fuels (or at least nuclear fission) while the rest of the world turns to solar and wind power.

Regarding guns, many Americans believe that the Second Amendment to the Constitution – the right to bear arms – is aimed at giving citizens the freedom to arm themselves to the teeth without regulation or formality. Generally, the Left is for some form of gun control, from small measures such as licensing and background checks for buyers to 'extreme' ones such as banning certain classes of weapon. Some might argue that the banning of military-style automatics has prevented the kind of mass shootings the US has become famous for from occurring more frequently in places like Australia, Canada and the UK, but the political right see any attempt at regulating firearms as a slippery slope to disarming the populace and leaving the people vulnerable to tyranny on the government's part. Tyranny for them means free healthcare by the way.

On religion, the Left generally supports freedom for all creeds, freedom of worship and freedom from discrimination based on religion. It also would like to keep the church and state separated and keep religion out of the education system and public schools. This one is very much in line with the tenets of the Constitution, of which the Right purports to be devout followers. It is also ironic that on this topic the Right agrees in principle, but only wants freedom for its own religion – Christianity. It would also like to see its religion taught (or perhaps enforced) in the school curriculum and measures taken to restrict other religions, especially Islam, that range from the 'mild' monitoring of Muslims in case of ties to extremism to the draconian policy of banning them all from the country.

The Christian Bible, strictly speaking, also frowns upon homosexuality. However, Christ did say we should love our neighbors and that surely means forgiving the gays as well. The Right has pushed back against efforts to end discrimination against the LGBT community on much the same grounds as it did the black community or other minorities. Evangelicals have opposed gay marriage initiatives and even raised their own counter-concerns, for example trying to pass laws in several states that force transgender women to return to the men's bathrooms in public places. This is done under the guise of protecting 'family values'. As comedian Bill Maher quipped, 'Whenever I hear the word 'family' in the title, I think 'bigot''.

Perhaps the longest and most often discriminated group in the world is women. The US was later than many other countries in granting women the vote and until recently lagged severely in female representation in politics. There has been a surge however in the last two decades, thanks in part to the efforts of iconic figures such as Former First lady, New York Senator and Secretary of State Hillary Rodham Clinton, who was the Democratic Party's 2016 nominee and opponent of the Republican's misogynistic choice of Donald Trump. The Republicans have generally erred towards traditional ideals of womanhood, such as raising children and doing the housework. At least if you're an attractive blonde you have a future on cable news talk shows; but other than that, they would prefer women to be seen and not heard. They have also resisted legislation to end harassment in the workplace, ensure equal pay, and crucially to give women access to family planning services and abortions. The Trump administration has even shot down legislation aimed at protecting women from domestic violence. These are all items placed highly on the Democrats' platform, more so perhaps since choosing their first woman presidential nominee.

Welfare remains an economic sticking point. Regardless of the fact that Medicare and Medicaid – two programs that help the elderly and unemployed – are two of the biggest government programs, and that like most welfare programs and indeed federal handouts, the recipients are disproportionately found in red states, it is the Republican Party that wants benefits cut. The party has so far been very successful in getting constituents to vote against their own interests: convincing red-state dwellers that any kind of welfare is 'communism' and promising to make cuts in general while retaining just enough of the programs to keep their base afloat. The idea of welfare is abhorrent to them and they believe that most forms are simply the Democrats handing out money to minorities. That is, they are happy to see their tax dollars wasted on shiny new warships and stealth bombers, but can't stand the idea of a single cent going to poor black people, or 'families'.

Their Christian charity does not extend to immigrants either. A quick Google search reveals at least two dozen Bible verses about welcoming migrants, including Deuteronomy's 'The alien who resides among you shall be to you as a citizen,' and Christ's own quote from the book of Matthew, 'I was hungry and you gave me food, I was thirsty and you gave me drink, I was a stranger and you welcomed me.' Yeah, no. Every so often the Republicans tend to go on a pogrom against illegal immigrants who are mostly Hispanics from Latin America and have a darker hue of skin than the white Republican ideal. Although illegal immigrants only total about 11 million people, most actually work and they do the hard, manual and low-paying jobs that white Americans won't. The Right commonly rails against benefits being paid to the handful of migrants that can wrangle them in the few places that allow it, and the idea that Hispanics tend to veer towards crime, drugs and prostitution more than other groups. However by percentage, an illegal immigrant is less likely than a natural-born citizen to commit a crime of any sort. Nevertheless, the mere fact that big tent Democrats are more inclusive by nature and more likely to cut ethnic minorities a little slack is enough in itself to cause the two parties to be at loggerheads over immigration.

So it is for the Muslims. Since the September 11, 2001 terror attack and several subsequent wars in the Middle East, the US has become increasingly leery of anyone named Mohammed, Aisha or Hussein. The Republican Right, never a fan of foreigners, has found a new enemy and tends to push the notion that all Muslims are terrorists: guilt by association. It also created new battle lines with the Democrats and progressives, who tend to seek understanding and ask that all Muslims not be painted with such a broad brush. For the white Right, such inclusiveness is dangerous complacency that the brown terrorists will exploit to harm Americans. The notions that Muslims are a threat and that Obama is not American still hold broad appeal among evangelicals. It does not help President Obama in their eyes that his middle name is Hussein and that his mother had relationships with two Muslim men. The fact these men were darker-skinned foreigners (Obama's father was a Kenyan and later his stepfather, an Indonesian) of course had nothing to do with it, right?

Well it did. Because it brings us back to the perennial sticking point between the two parties: race. There is no escaping the fact that one party just likes minorities less. Republicans call blacks lazy; Democrats say they're disadvantaged. To Democrats the black community are often victims of irrational police violence; to the Republicans, provocateurs. To the Left and the world, Obama was a president who just happened to have Muslims in his family history; to the Right he is a potential Manchurian candidate, sent to infiltrate the White House and Islamize America.

Obama's election gave rise to the so-called 'Tea Party' an ultra-conservative faction of Republicans who, resenting the election of a black man to the nation's highest office, and burned by the recent crash of the housing market and subsequent recession, were looking for someone to blame. Somehow it was the incoming president's fault though the damage had already been done, and they took to the streets and soapboxes with calls for fiscal responsibility – meaning cuts to welfare programs of course. Despite the fact that the previous Republican administration under George W. Bush had reduced taxes and increased spending, indulged in two costly foreign wars and presided over the crash of the housing market, now that a black guy was in office, it was suddenly time to clean up the books. It would not be enough to criticize the president's financial policy, which of course included some public spending that they wouldn't approve of anyway. They had to go after him and demonize him on a level so personal that it would expose the racist white core of the GOP. The Tea Party Caucus as it was known were all white.

And here is where the evangelicals' old nemesis, race and their more recent pet cause abortion neatly dovetail. Yes, Trump has appointed the required slew of pro-life judges and red states have gone about tightening access to abortion and family planning. With a majority of state legislatures and both houses of Congress under Republican control, it is fair to say any Republican president could have pulled that off, and most would have. Yet, Trump beat out over a dozen Republican primary candidates, all with greater religious and conservative credentials, many with just as good a chance of beating the Democrats. There is more to just stopping abortion than the right to life. There's something else about Trump and Trumpism that appeals to the base.

It is said that over time adherents tend to impose their own values on religion that slowly displace its original tenets and become the new gospel. For the Conservative Right, the love that Christ preached for the poor, the downtrodden, the different has slowly given way to a new set of standards. These 'values' became racial superiority, inequality, intolerance, xenophobia; and Trump undoubtedly embodies these. After his 2020 loss, Trump embraced the conservative Heritage Foundation's so-called project 2025, a dystopian plan to remold America into a Christo-fascist nation after winning the next election. Among the project's aims, should Trump take the White House again, are a nationwide ban on abortion, limited access to contraception, imposing religious teaching in schools; paring back transgender rights, stacking the judiciary, banning marriage equality and the teaching of Critical Race Theory and firing much of the civil service to replace them with Trump loyalists. It probably reads better in the original German. Because Project 2025 is so unpopular with voters, Trump has sought to distance himself personally from the plan, yet he has filled campaign with its proponents, including Vice Presidential pick JD Vance.

America is slowly becoming a 'minority majority' nation, where most inhabitants are black, brown, Latino; Muslim, Jewish, Sikh or Hindu. White people, while still the largest single demographic, are due in a few years to be outnumbered by all the others – you know, those 'huddled masses' that the plaque talks about. Though the low birth rate among white couples is largely a symptom of prosperity (wealthy, educated families tend to have fewer children nowadays), the Christian Right believes the sexual liberation of the sixties, with easy access to contraception and easier licentiousness, culminated in the great immorality of Roe v. Wade at the Supreme Court. They blame women's choice – birth control, abortion, or just refusing to 'obey' their husbands 'in all things' as the Old Testament prescribes – for a dangerously low birth rate that threatens to displace their white majority. They see more babies as a path back to supremacy, conveniently ignoring the fact that fewer abortions and less access to contraception will probably cause even more 'brown' births: it is quite possible that if abortion were illegal and less common it wouldn't mean affluent white girls having more babies; just more poor people and immigrants with typically large families.

The solution to that, of course, is to deny minorities the vote, citizenship, legal rights, healthcare, advocacy and otherwise strip them of power. Evangelicals mostly only care about rights of the unborn. Once you're out of your mother's uterus folks, if you're poor, ethnic and colored, you're on your own. To that end, Evangelicals are more likely to stand against immigration, even to the point of believing silly rumors such as billionaire philanthropist George Soros sponsoring a migrant caravan intent on crashing the southern border. They're more likely to tune into Fox News to hear the latest updates about 'crime-ridden' Chicago. They are more likely to vote for federal judges and a Supreme Court that will restrict or ban abortion, which they see as threatening their social, political, economic and numerical supremacy. They're more prone to supporting a xenophobic strongman and in Donald Trump, they have found one.

The Trump Prophecy was a 2018 film released by an evangelical-funded production house that argued Trump was similar to the Biblical Cyrus the Great, a 6th Century B.C. Persian king and conqueror of Israel who, though a heathen and a sinner, nevertheless treated God's chosen people with surprising leniency and respect. They believe that Trump, though similarly flawed, was likewise sent by God to restore the religious 'liberty' of white American Christians – that is the freedom to discriminate against and oppress others in the name of God. White America wants to get back at New America for the crime of simply changing, and Trumpism is the vehicle. Since then we've seen him fail miserably at leading, enrich himself at the nation's expense, ignore a pandemic causing hundreds of thousands of excess deaths, attempt to steal an election then use the excuse to keep bilking his followers of their hard earned cash and finally attempt to rinse and repeat it all with a new election run.

Trump's religious followers do not care at all that his business dealings have been one long series of frauds, his personal relationships a mess of affairs and divorces, that his divisive presidency corruptly fleeced the public coffers as it failed to even attempt to 'unite' the world (or even the country) as promised. As long as he keeps holding up The Other to hate, he has their support. When discussing the tactics of his segregationist rivals in the sixties, Lyndon Johnson explained, 'If you can convince the lowest white man he's better than the best colored man, he won't notice you're picking his pocket. Give him someone to look down on and he'll empty his pockets for you.'

So far over seventy million Americans are lining up to hand over the contents of their pockets to a megalomaniac with a silly hairdo and a fake tan, for precisely that reason.

SELECTED READING

Foreword

Evans, C.J. (2009). White Evangelical Protestant Responses To The Civil Rights Movement. *The Harvard Theological Review*: 102 (2); 245-273

Fea, J. (2018). *Believe Me: The Evangelical Road To Donald Trump.* Grand Rapids: Eerdmans Publishing

Green, E. (2014). The Evangelical Slide On Immigration Reform. *The Atlantic: 2014, Jun 11*

Schwadel, P., & Smith, G.A. (2019). <u>Evangelical Approval Of Trump Remains High, But Other Religious Groups Are Less Supportive</u>. *Pew Research Center.*

1. Thou shalt worship no other gods before Me

Bergen, P., & Smith, N.G. (2019). Trump and His Generals: The Cost of Chaos. Penguin Audio

Dale, D. (2024). *Fact check: Trump revives lie that he was long ago named 'Man of the Year' in Michigan.* CNN, June 16.

D'Angelo, T. (2024). *Donald Trump claims two more golf championships; Jack Nicklaus presents him with 'most improved player' award.* Palm Beach Post, March 17.

Dreier, P. (2019). Why Trump Keeps Telling the World 'I'm Smart'. Prospect.org

Levin, B. (2019). Trump insists he's smart enough to commit crimes. *Vanity fair*

Milman, O. (2019). Trump administration's war on science has hit 'crisis point', experts warn. *The Guardian*

Rucker, P., & Leonnig, C. (2020) *A Very Stable Genius: Donald J. Trump's Testing of America*. Penguin Random House

Rumford, J. (2018). *Tobacco, Trusts, and Trump: How America's Forgotten War Created Big Government*

Wolff, M. (2018). Fire and Fury: Inside the Trump White House. London: Little Brown

Wolters, E., & Steel, B. (2018). *When Ideology Trumps Science: Why We Question the Experts on Everything from Climate Change to Vaccinations*. Santa Barbara: Praeger

2. Thou shalt not bow to any graven image

Burns, M. (2021). *Golden Trump statue at CPAC implies he's king of the GOP. But his position isn't secure*. NBC News, February 26.

Enrich, D. (2020). *Dark Towers: Deutsche Bank, Donald Trump, and an Epic Trail of Destruction*. New York: HarperCollins

Harold, C.N., & Nelson, L.P. (2018). *Charlottesville 2017: The Legacy of Race and Inequity*. University of Virginia Press

Hettena, S. (2018). *Trump / Russia: A Definitive History*. New York: Melville House

The Nation. (2017). *Trump and the NRA - Arming the Culture War Has Just Begun*. The Nation: 2017, July 17

Robbins, J.W., & Crockett, C. (2018). *Doing Theology in the Age of Trump: A Critical Report on Christian Nationalism*. Eugene: Wipf & Stock

Spencer, H. (2018). *Summer of Hate: Charlottesville, USA*. University of Virginia Press

Stanger, A. (2019). *Whistleblowers: Honesty in America from Washington to Trump*. Yale University Press

3.   Thou shalt not take the name of the Lord in vain.

Denker, A. (2019). *Red State Christians: Understanding the Voters Who Elected Donald Trump*. Minneapolis: Fortress Press

Hassan, S. (2019).*The Cult of Trump: A Leading Cult Expert Explains How the President Uses Mind Control*. New York: Simon & Schuster

Marti, G. (2020). *American Blindspot: Race, Class, Religion, and the Trump Presidency.* New York: Rowman & Lyttlefield

Olmsted, E. (2024). *Trump's Black Church stunt was bad. His next event was even worse.* The New Republic 19 June, 2024.

Patrice, J. (2024) *$60 Trump Bibles Include US Constitution…minus all the equal protection and presidential term limits.* AboveTheLaw.com, May16 2024

Posner, S. (2008). *God's Profits: Faith, Fraud, and the Republican Crusade for Values Voters*. Sausalito, CA: PoliPointPress

4.   Thou shalt keep the Sabbath holy

Cranley, E. (2019). *Inside Trump's daily routine, which includes 3 to 4 hours of sleep, 'executive time,' and no breakfast. Business Insider:* 2019, Feb 10.

Germain, S. (2020) Trump Golf Count [Web page].

Jones, C. (2019). *Trump's Golf Trips Could Cost Taxpayers Over $340 Million*. Forbes: 2019, Jul 10.

Moroz, H. (2018). *The Book of Tweets: President Trump's Social Media Revolution & America's New Birth of Freedom*. United States: Moroz Law

Oppenheim, M. (2019). *Donald Trump's reported TV habits would 'get most Americans sacked'*. The Independent: 2017, Dec 10.

Woodward, B. (2018). *Fear: Trump in the White House*. New York: Simon & Schuster.

5.   Honor thy Father and thy Mother

Bernstein, A. (2019). *American Oligarchs: The Kushners, the Trumps, and the Marriage of Money and Power*. New York: W.W. Norton

Blair, G. (2001). *The Trumps: Three Generations of Builders and a President*. New York: Simon & Schuster

Cay Johnston, D. (2016). *The Making of Donald Trump. New York*: Melville House

Fahrenthold, D. A. (2017). *Uncovering Trump: The Truth Behind Donald Trump's Charitable Giving*. New York: Diversion Books

Kennedy, M. (2019). *Judge Says Trump Must Pay $2 Million Over Misuse Of Foundation Funds*. NPR: 2017, Nov 7

Tangalakis-lippert, K., & Zavarise, I. (2022). *Ivana Trump was buried near the first hole of Trump National Golf Club. Her gravesite could offer tax breaks for the business*. Business Insider, July 31.

Wolffe, R. (2019). Why did Trump say his dad was German? He lies so much he doesn't know the truth. The Guardian: 2019, Apr 4

6. Thou shalt not kill

Bethea, C. (2019). *Trump the accomplice: El Paso residents blame the president for a hate-fuelled mass shooting.* The New Yorker: 2019, Aug 5

Davis, J.H., & Shear, M.D. (2019). *Border Wars: Inside Trump's Assault on Immigration.* New York: Simon & Schuster

Friend, A., Karlin, M., & DeJonge Schulman, L. (2020). *Why did the Pentagon ever give Trump the option of killing Soleimani?* The Brookings Institution, 2020, Jan 14

Fuchs, M.H. (2019). *The American right wing is enabling a dual crisis: gun violence and white supremacy.* The Guardian: 2019, Aug 7

Gilsinan, K. (2019). *Trump Is Killing a Fatally Flawed Syria Policy.* The Atlantic: 2019, Oct 8

Kassie, E. (2019). *Detained: How the US built the World's largest immigrant detention system.* The Guardian: 2019, Sep 24

Jansen, B. (2019). *Trump administration announces plan that would let it detain undocumented children indefinitely.* USA Today: 2019, Aug 21

Lewis, W.C. (2019). *New Policies in Middle East but Same Wars –Trump, Obama, Assad, Putin and Syria.*

McManus, D. (2024). *Trump Lionizes Jan 6 Rioters as 'Warriors.' Could the Dog Whistle be any Louder?* The Los Angeles Times 17 June, 2024

Tanfani, J., Parker, N., and Eisler, P. (2024). *Judges in Trump Related Cases Face Unprecedented Wave of Threats:* Reuters, 2024 February 29

The Nation. (2017). *Trump and the NRA - Arming the Culture War Has Just Begun*: The Nation July 17/24, 2017

7. Thou shalt not commit adultery

Allen, J., & Stempel, J. (2019). FBI documents point to Trump role in hush money for porn star Daniels. *Reuters: 2019, Jul 18*

Daniels, S. (2018). *Full Disclosure*. United Kingdom: St Martin's Press

Farrow, R. (2019). *Catch and Kill: Lies, Spies, and a Conspiracy to Protect Predators*. New York: Little, Brown & Company

Haelle, T. (2017). Man Boasts Of Sexual Assault, Later Inaugurated 45th President Of United States. *Forbes: 2017, Jan 20*

Levine, B., & El-Faizy, M. (2019). *All the President's Women: Donald Trump and the Making of a Predator*. New York: Hachette Books

Newsweek. (2024 Apr 9). Map Shows 12 States That Allow Child Marriage After Virginia Passes Law [web page]

Relman, E. (2018). The 25 women who have accused Trump of sexual misconduct. *Business Insider: 2017, Dec 22*

Tolentino, J. (2016). Trump And The Truth: The Sexual-Assault Allegations. *The New Yorker: 2016, Oct 20*

8. Thou shalt not steal

American Civil Liberties Union. (2020). Fighting Voter Suppression [web page].

Anderson, C. (2019). *One Person, No Vote: How Voter Suppression Is Destroying Our Democracy*. New York: Bloomsbury Publishing

Beer, T. (2021). *Trump Campaign Reportedly Forced To Refund More Than $122 Million To Donors*. Forbes, April 3, 2021

The Brennan Center for Justice. (2007-2019). The Myth of Voter Fraud [web page].

Cay Johnston, D. (2016). *The Making of Donald Trump. New York*: Melville House

Daniels, G.R. (2020).*Uncounted: The Crisis of Voter Suppression in America*. New York University Press

Derysh, I. (2020). Voter suppression plain and simple: Texas closed hundreds of polling sites in Black, Latino areas. *Salon: 2020, March 3.*

Durkin richer, A. (2023). *The Election Meddling Indictment Against Trump Is Sprawling: Here's A Breakdown Of The Case.* Associated Press, August 2, 2023

Fein, R., Bonifaz, J., & Clemens B. (2018). *The Constitution Demands It: The Case for the Impeachment of Donald Trump.* New York: Melville House.

Isikoff, M., & Corn, D. (2018). *Russian Roulette: The Inside Story of Putin's War on America and the Election of Donald Trump.* New York: Twelve Publishing

Jacobs, R., & McGuire, R. (2023). *Trump Made Up To $160 Million From Foreign Countries As President.* Citizens For Ethics

Kranish, M. (2017). *Trump Revealed: The Definitive Biography of the 45th President.* New York: Scribner

Mueller, R. S. (2019). *Report On The Investigation Into Russian Interference In The 2016 Presidential Election.* Department of Justice

Piklington, E., (2022) . *The big rip-ff: How Trump exploited his fans with election defense fund.* The Guardian, June 18, 2022

Schwarz, B. (2024). *Trump And His Favorite Fundraising Platform Both Face Donor Problems.* CNBC 26 February 2024

Thomsen, J., Lynch, S., & Goudsward, A. (2023) *Explainer: who allegedly conspired with Trump to overturn the 2020 election?* Reuters, August 2, 2023

Unger, C. (2019). *House of Trump, House of Putin: The Untold Story of Donald Trump and the Russian Mafia.* New York: Random House

Zirin, J.D. (2018).Plaintiff in Chief: A Portrait of Donald Trump in 3,500 Lawsuits. New York: All Points Books

9. Thou shalt not bear false witness

Cay Johnston, D. (2016). *The Making Of Donald Trump. New York*: Melville House

Carpenter, A. (2018). *Gaslighting America: Why We Love It When Trump Lies To Us*. Broadside Books

Dyson, M.E. (2016). *The Black Presidency: Barack Obama And The Politics Of Race In America*. New York: Houghton Mifflin Harcourt

Jardina, A., & Traugott, M. (2019). The Genesis Of The Birther Rumor: Partisanship, Racial Attitudes, And Political Knowledge. *The Journal Of Race, Ethnicity, And Politics: 4 (1)*

McGraw, M. (2022). *Trump's election fraud claims were false. Here are his advisers who said so*. Politico, June 13.

Marley, P. (2020). *Wisconsin Supreme Court upholds Biden's win, rejects Trump lawsuit*. Milwaukee Journal Sentinel, December 14.

Neumeister, L., pelz, J., & Sisak, M. (2023). *Jury finds Trump liable for sexual abuse, awards accuser $5M*. Associated Press, May 10.

Offenhartz, J. (2024). *Trump ordered to pay additional $83.3 million to E. Jean Carroll in defamation case*. NPR, January 26.

Olmsted, E. (2024). *New Report Details Terrifying Threat of Trump's Election Deniers*. The New Republic, July 30.

Reeve, E. (2012). A Case Study In The Evolution Of Birtherism: Donald Trump. *The Atlantic: 2012, May 25*

Romo, V. (2020). *Wisconsin Supreme Court Rules Trump Election Challenge 'Unreasonable In The Extreme.'* NPR, December 14.

Rucker, P., & Leonnig, C. (2020) *A Very Stable Genius: Donald J. Trump's Testing Of America*. Penguin Random House

Stempel, J. (2024). *Trump formally ordered to pay $454 million in New York fraud case*. Reuters, February 24.

Walker, J. (2013). *The United States Of Paranoia: A Conspiracy Theory.* New York: Harpercollins

Washington Post, (2021). Trump claims database. *In four years, President Trump made 30,543 false or misleading claims.*

Wilson, T. (2024). *Trump ordered to pay $83 million in E. Jean Carroll verdict.* USA Today, January 29.

10. Thou shalt not covet

The Washington Post. (2018). *Donald Trump's 'dictator envy' on full display in latest praise for North Korean leader Kim Jong-un. SCMP:* 2018, Jun 16

Robinson, R. (2018). *What's Up with Trump's Obama Envy?* Newsday: 2019, Sep 1

Oprysko, C. (2019). *Trump claims Nobel Peace Prize is rigged against him.* Politico: 2019, Sep 23

Sheffield, M. (2018). *Donald Trump's creepy comments about daughter Ivanka: A history.* Salon: 2018, Mar 23

Walt, S.M. (2019). *Trump's Shameless Path to the Nobel Peace Prize.* Foreign Policy: 2019, Sep 23

Haraldsson, H. (2016). *The Grotesque History of Donald Trump's Sexual Comments About His Daughter.* Politics USA: 2016, Oct 8

Crockett, E. (2016). *Donald Trump has been making disturbing comments about young girls for years.* Vox: 2016, Oct 18

Epilogue

Benen, S. (2024). *Trump responds to Biden announcement in a decidedly Trumpian way.* MSNBC, Jul 22

Evans, C.J. (2009). White Evangelical Protestant Responses to the Civil Rights Movement. *The Harvard Theological Review*: 102 (2); 245-273

Fea, J. (2018). *Believe Me: The Evangelical Road to Donald Trump*. Grand Rapids: Eerdmans Publishing

Hacker, J. S., & Pierson, P. (2020). *Let them Eat Tweets: How the Right Rules in an Age of Extreme Inequality*. New York: Liveright

Lynton, C., & Watson, K. (2024). *Biden makes statement after Trump rally shooting*. CBS news, July 13.

Mamrak, R. (2018). *TRUMP: Evangelical Plague*. Pin Oak Bottom Press

Maxwell, A. (2019). *The Long Southern Strategy: How Chasing White Voters in the South Changed American Politics*. Oxford University Press

Stevens, S. (2020). *It Was All a Lie: How the Republican Party Became Donald Trump*. New York: Doubleday

www.ingramcontent.com/pod-product-compliance
Lightning Source LLC
Chambersburg PA
CBHW031053250726
48655CB00004B/1414